H. H. Eddy

BELGIUM

AND

WESTERN GERMANY

IN

1833;

INCLUDING VISITS

TO

BADEN-BADEN, WIESBADEN, CASSEL, HANOVER,
THE HARZ MOUNTAINS, &c. &c.

By Mrs. TROLLOPE,

AUTHOR OF "DOMESTIC MANNERS OF THE AMERICANS."

TWO VOLUMES.

VOL. I.

THE SECOND EDITION.

LONDON:
JOHN MURRAY, ALBEMARLE-STREET.
MDCCCXXXV.

Windham Press is committed to bringing the lost cultural heritage of ages past into the 21st century through high-quality reproductions of original, classic printed works at affordable prices.

This book has been carefully crafted to utilize the original images of antique books rather than error-prone OCR text. This also preserves the work of the original typesetters of these classics, unknown craftsmen who laid out the text, often by hand, of each and every page you will read. Their subtle art involving judgment and interaction with the text is in many ways superior and more human than the mechanical methods utilized today, and gave each book a unique, hand-crafted feel in its text that connected the reader organically to the art of bindery and book-making.

We think these benefits are worth the occasional imperfection resulting from the age of these books at the time of scanning, and their vintage feel provides a connection to the past that goes beyond the mere words of the text.

As bibliophiles, we are always seeking perfection in our work, so please notify us of any errors in this book by emailing us at corrections@windhampress.com. Our team is motivated to correct errors quickly so future customers are better served. Our mission is to raise the bar of quality for reprinted works by a focus on detail and quality over mass production. To peruse our catalog of carefully curated classic works, please visit our online store at www.windhampress.com.

CONTENTS

OF

VOLUME THE FIRST.

Chapter I.

Page

Lord Liverpool Steam-boat—Private Theatricals—Military Mass—Ghistelles—Jabbeke—Oudenbourg—Flemish Farm-house—Fête-Dieu—M. Paret—Bruges—M. Moke—Hospital of St. John—Jerusalem Chapel—Marché au Vendredi—Hôtel de Commerce 1

Chapter II.

Ghent—Antiquities—St. Bavon—The University—Schamp's Collection—Bull Fight—Espions—Beguinage—St. Michael's—Antwerp—Spanish Air—Effects of the Siege 30

Chapter III.

Antwerp—Notre Dame—Rubens—Academy—Vandyke—Calvary—Passports—Voitures—Arrival at Brussels—Belgian Politics—M. Alexandre Rodenbach—Chamber of Representatives—Duel—Society—Palace of the Prince of Orange—Mint—MM. Vandermaelen—M. Robyns—Du Bos—Theatre—St. Gudule—Old Town—Louvain—Tervueren—Dilapidations—Tree of Liberty 50

Chapter IV.

Waterloo—St. Jean—Belle Alliance—Monuments—Road to Namur—Namur—Huy—Pensionnat—Citadel—Liege—Quentin Durward—Churches—Chaudfontaine—Belgian Politics . . 83

Chapter V.

Aix-la-Chapelle—Charlemagne—Napoleon—Relics—King of Prussia—German Politics . 118

Chapter VI.

Journey to Cologne—Reasons for Travelling—The Cathedral—Museum—Public Walks—Music—Bonn—Concert—Students—Smoking . . 132

Chapter VII.

Godesberg—The Seven Hills—Drachenfels—Friesdorf—Stromberg—Catholic Devotion—Kreutzberg—Buried Monks—Table-d'hôte—German Manners—Unkel—Laacher-see . . . 154

Chapter VIII.

Rolandseck — Orlando Furioso — Nonnenwert — Unkel — Neuwied — Coblentz — The Moselle — Steam-boat Passengers — Mayence . . 193

Chapter IX.

Mayence—Cathedral—Francfort—Theatre—Cathedral—St. Catherine's—Cemetery—Jewish Synagogue—Luther—Hesse Hombourg . . 222

Chapter X.

Darmstadt—Heppenheim—Storkenberg—Bergstrasse—Weinheim—Peasantry—Crops—Mannheim—The Palace—Ducal Gardens—Ball—Observatory—Church of the Jesuits—Theatre—Schwetzingen Gardens 260

Chapter XI.

Heidelberg—Neuenheim—Heidelberg Castle—The Necker—Neckersteinach—Tilsberg—Steinach—Tun of Heidelberg—Broken Tower—English Antiquaries 287

☞ The Sketches by Mr. Hervieu, so frequently alluded to in the following pages, were intended to accompany this publication; but the expense of engraving them in the style they deserved was found so great, that the idea was abandoned.

PREFACE.

"Is it possible," said a friend, who entered my room one day, when I was sitting before a table covered with note-books, scraps of memoranda, sketches, and relics of all I had seen and heard from the 1st of June to the 15th of September, 1833—"Is it possible that you mean to publish anything upon your summer tour?"

"Yes," I replied:—"I mean forthwith to tell all about it, in print."

"Have you considered," rejoined my friend, "that every inch of ground which you have travelled over has been described a hundred times already? . . . . Must not all that can be said upon it now, be as tedious as a ten times told tale? Trust me, ground so beaten must be dangerous ground. Those who would write novels must take the trouble of going farther a-field.—Arabia, or Egypt, might, perhaps, furnish details worth reading; but—for your summer tour! ! . . I really hope you will give up the idea."

"Your remonstrance appears so fearfully reasonable," said I, "that I doubt if it be possible to set it fairly aside . . . . and yet . . ."

My friend rose and took his hat.

"I understand you," said he;—" you know I am right, *and yet,* you are determined to have your own way."

So saying, he shook his head, shrugged his shoulders, and left me.

I put my papers aside—pushed my desk away, and sat meditating upon the counsel I had received. There was, unquestionably, much truth in it, *and yet*—for the pertinacious *yet* would not leave me—I did not abandon the idea of publishing my notes.

Nevertheless, I remitted the test of transcribing till I had found reasons sufficient, at least to satisfy myself that it was possible a new book on an old subject might win readers.

My little volumes on America have been much read .... Many have said that this was owing to their being written with strong party feeling; but I—who am in the secret—know that such was not the case. The cause of their success, therefore, must be sought elsewhere; and I attribute it solely to that intuitive power of discerning what is written with truth, which is possessed, often unconsciously, by every reader.

Be he pleased or displeased by the pictures brought before him, he feels that the images portrayed are real, and this will interest, even if it vex him.

I have an inveterate habit of suffering all I see to make a deep impression on my memory, and the result of this is, a sort of mosaic, by no means very grand in outline or skilful in drawing; but each morsel of colour has the deep reality of truth, in which there is ever some value; and it is on this, and this alone, I rest my hope that the following pages may be acceptable to the public.

BELGIUM

AND

WESTERN GERMANY

In 1833.

Chapter I.

Lord Liverpool Steam-boat—Private Theatricals—Military Mass— Ghistelles—Jabbeke — Oudenbourg— Flemish Farm-house—Fête-Dieu—M. Paret—Bruges —M. Moke—Hospital of St. John—Jerusalem Chapel—Marché au Vendredi—Hôtel de Commerce.

I LEFT London for Ostend on the 1st of June, accompanied by my son and Mr. H——. The weather was delightful, and we had several agreeable fellow-passengers, but I should have been sorely vexed had I spied any transatlantic acquaintance among them; for, in truth, a comparison between the accommodation on board the Lord Liverpool packet, and that which is found in all and every of the unnumbered steam-boats of the United

States, would have redounded very little to the honour of our steam-establishment.

The vessel was dirty, and the fare both bad and insufficient. Had any accident detained us, even for a few hours, the passengers, among whom there were many children, must have suffered very seriously from want of provision; for after the three o'clock dinner, not an atom of bread, or even biscuit, remained on board.

We reached Ostend a little after midnight, and found very comfortable rooms bespoken for us at the Waterloo Hotel. Notwithstanding the uncouth hour, we sat down to a meal, wherein supper was at odds with breakfast, as to which it might be called; but it was rendered extremely welcome by the previous fast.

It was my purpose to pass a few days at Ostend, both for the sake of enjoying the society of some friends residing there, and because my son had engaged to take a part in the representation of a comedy, which was to be performed by a party of English amateurs, who had amused themselves for some days before our arrival in preparing it. This comedy (She Stoops to Conquer) was extremely well got up, and performed with a great deal of spirit and cleverness; but it was followed by a farce, which very nearly proved a tragedy. This unlucky farce (Bombastes Furioso) has a single combat in the last scene, and my son was wounded severely in the thigh, by a thrust from the sword of his adversary. This unlucky accident stretched our intended three days' stay to ten; but fortunately produced no lasting inconvenience to the wounded hero.

Few tourists pause more than an hour or two at Ostend : it is passed through merely as a doorway, by which to enter the interesting country of which it is the frontier. I will not say that my residence of ten days taught me to find beauty in the sandy level on which the town stands; but it enabled me to discover that, as a bathing-place, it has many advantages.

As a sea walk, the Levée, which is raised before the fortifications, and passes on for a mile beyond them, is delightful. In addition to its fine seaview, it has the attraction of the elegant pavilion recently built upon it under the superintendence of the British Consul. This pretty edifice, which commands a noble marine view, is fitted up with great taste for the rest and amusement of the loungers. It contains rooms for reading, refreshments, and raffling; and is altogether as agreeable a resort as any bathing-place I have seen can boast.

There is another circumstance at Ostend, which I consider very important as one of the *agrémens* of a summer residence; it has a cheap and most abundant market for vegetables, fruit, and flowers, which perhaps struck me the more, from my having so often experienced the want of these luxuries at our own watering-places.

Henry's wound, though it confined him to his bed, in no respect affected his general health, and the tedious restraint was alleviated by books, and the visits of many who were kind enough to take pity on his seclusion. Among these was his young adversary, whose constant attention showed a very amiable degree of regret for the unlucky accident.

With such excellent substitutes to take my place, I felt no scruple at leaving him; and found time to see all that Ostend has to show.

On Sunday I attended mass at the fine old church of St. Peter. The pulpit, confessionals, and stalls are superbly carved. There is no great architectural beauty in the building; but each of the three aisles is terminated by a very handsome altar. It was vexing to my reformed eyes, to see one of these profaned by a huge wooden doll, with a fine watch at her side, and dressed in satins and lace, intended to represent the Virgin. Its draperies and decorations had just been refreshed and renewed, in preparation for the *Fête-Dieu*, which was to take place on the following Sunday. Nothing could be more childishly grotesque than this figure; yet I was touched by the unmistakeable devotion of a poor old woman, who kneeled on the pavement before it. Her withered arms were extended, and an air of the most passionate adoration animated her sunken features, as she gazed on this frightful idol. —And after all, perhaps, there is something sublime in the state of mind, which allows not the senses to dwell on the object before them, but, occupied alone by the holiness of the symbol, is raised by it to such thoughts of heaven, as chase all feelings but those of devotion. That this is often the case with sincere Roman Catholics I have no doubt; and it is impossible to witness the feeling, without losing all inclination to ridicule the source of it.

After the first service was concluded, we remained in the church to witness that most incongruous medley of sights and sounds, a military mass. I was well pleased to be present at a ceremony so perfectly new to me; but it hovered so strangely between the sublime and the ridiculous, that it would be difficult to describe its effect. The measured tread of the long lines of soldiery reverberating along the lofty aisles, and the subdued, serious look that quenched their martial bearing, as they ranged themselves in triple file round the building, were solemn and impressive; but when the grim and grotesque *sapeurs*, accompanied by the whole band, marched up to the very steps of the altar, which they seemed to besiege with their thundering drums and trumpets, I knew not how to fancy the ceremony a religious one.

The next day was spent in an excursion with a very agreeable pic-nic party, to show us something of the neighbouring country. We first drove to Ghistelles, a pretty village with a handsome church. The most interesting object in it is a monument erected to a certain Countess Godeliève, who was barbarously murdered by command of her husband, some few hundred years ago, and is now worshipped as a saint. Her stately monument, indeed, might, with more propriety, be termed an altar, for the lower part of it is arranged as such, and beside it is a shrine of brass, containing the bones of the strangled lady, before which a lamp is kept burning day and night. In the highest compartment of this monumental altar is a group of three figures, which even at that height appear as large as life. This composition represents the manner of the murder, which was performed by strangulation. A cord appears to be twisted round the neck of the kneeling female, either end of which is in the hand of a ruffian, who is represented as putting forth his whole strength to complete the work. The attitude of one of these, who seems to be pressing his knee against the victim, to obtain a better purchase for his pull, is horribly true to nature. They sell a little book in the church containing St. Godeliève's legend, her litany, and some account of her miracles. The following is a translation of the legend:—

"Godeliève was a woman of France, and married a baron of Flanders, who, being a very wicked man, and influenced by a still more atrocious mother, hated her for her goodness, and also for having black hair, unlike the fair girls of his own country. He, therefore, had her strangled, but afterwards repenting him of the cruel deed, he became a monk at Bruges, and subsequently caused this church to be erected to her memory."

I do not find the name of this saint in the calendar, but the miracles recorded to her honour are numerous, and some of no distant date. A lively Swiss lady, who was one of our pic-nic, told me that a saint of older standing, who had also an altar in the church, had felt himself much offended by the superior devotion manifested for the parvenue St. Godelième. How this displeasure was made known I did not learn; but the Curé informed his parishioners that some relics of this older saint were certainly concealed near Ghistelles. Accordingly a day was chosen, on which he set out at the head of all the faithful to seek for them. They went about and about for many hours, but found nothing; at length the Curé declared that he could go no farther, for his limbs refused to support him; and so saying, he stretched himself on the earth. After some time, he again attempted to proceed; but was still unable to move. " My children," he repeated, " I can go no farther;—search here, even here, where my strength failed me." They did so—and, wonderful to tell, found a finger-bone exactly at the spot where the pious man had laid him down to rest.

This well-authenticated finger of the saint was conveyed to his altar, and enshrined with all the observant devotion for which *les braves Belges* are so justly celebrated. It has already wrought many wonderful miracles; and, to use the words of our bright-eyed chronicler, "La pauvre Ste. Godelièvè a perdu la plus grande partie de sa pratique."

Close to the church is the site of the old castle of Ghistelles, and some trifling remains of the building may yet be traced.

The prison of the little town is under the same roof as the hotel; a vicinity which would render any long sojourn there far from agreeable. We saw two very wretched countenances glaring upon us through the bars, at the distance of a few feet, as we passed from the door to the carriage.

From Ghistelles we proceeded to Jabbeke, where the Baron von Larebeke has a very handsome residence. Like all old mansions of the noblesse in that country, it has its tower and its moat. The gardens are large and very full of roses, which seem to flourish to perfection in the sandy soil; but unfortunately wooden effigies of men and women, painted proper, as heralds call it, were almost equally abundant. Some of these groups are much too strange for description.

The baron was absent, but we were permitted to see the château. It contains several handsome apartments, and a gallery of pictures, among which are some few originals of the Flemish, and many copies of the Italian schools. Having amused ourselves here till we were a little tired, and very hungry, we walked back to the inn, where we had left the carriage; and sat down to a repast, agreeable in every way.

We returned to Ostend by a different route, that took us through Oudenbourg for the purpose of seeing some of the highly cultivated gardens which supply the Ostend market; and also to visit a farm belonging to a relation of one of our party, which showed us an excellent specimen of the interior of a Flemish farm-house. The extremest cleanliness, the kindest civility, and a magnificent display of rich cream and Valenciennes lace, were among its most remarkable features. We observed also many indications of devout Catholicism. Dolls superbly dressed, with lesser dolls pinned to their stomachers, to represent the Virgin and Child, and crucifixes of various dimensions, were displayed in seven different nooks of the principal apartment.

This room, which was very large, had a neat

curtained bed. Its snow-white quilt and nicely flounced pillows looked as if it were intended only for show. We saw, however, in the kitchen, and other inferior rooms, preparations for sleeping less delicately, the beds being laid literally in cupboards ranged against the walls.

Our lovely Swiss friend coaxed the good woman of the house to exhibit the stays she wore on great occasions. They were unquestionably of many pounds' weight; and were furnished on both sides with iron bars, which, one should think, must enter, if not into her soul, at least into her heart, every time she stooped. An examination of this machine enabled me to comprehend the meaning of a term in common use among us. I have often felt at a loss to know why a lady's corset should be termed " *a pair of stays ;*" but with this massive fabric before me, I at once perceived its origin and meaning. Ribs of steel are enclosed within it on either side, and it could hardly be better described than by calling it a pair of stays, or supports. About half way down the sides of this ponderous structure is a huge solid roll of stuffing, which nearly surrounds the waist, and on this the petticoats are suspended.

After a full examination of this "foreign wonder," we were shown many singularly-fashioned caps, bordered by the most delicate lace. Though the whole establishment had an air of comfort and plenty about it, the costly elegance of these decorations surprised me. But it was easy to perceive that a feeling of family dignity was attached to them. The blooming daughters of the house, whose bright hair had never yet been shaded by anything beyond a ribbon, listened to our expressions of admiration, which were carefully interpreted, with much such satisfaction as the daughter of a baron might feel if her paternal castle were the theme of praise.

The dairy at this house was really a beautiful sight, even though at one end of it we perceived a nymph skimming cream with her fingers. This, indeed, is the universal method; and if anything could reconcile one to the strange operation, it would be the delicate rosy tips of the Rubens-like fingers we saw so employed.

I have never in any country remarked finer crops than in the sandy plain round Ostend. The mode of husbandry is careful and laborious; but the returns are very great. The constant application of manure converts the arid soil into a fine loam; and every inch of it is as carefully weeded as the nicest garden. This fatiguing but necessary part of good husbandry is performed chiefly by women, who crawl along the ground on their hands and knees, and in this attitude appear to draw the weeds more effectually, and with less labour, than can be done by stooping.

The ploughing of this district is, as may be supposed, peculiarly light; and is often performed by a single milch cow. No part of Flemish farming appeared to me more worthy of attention than the general management of their cows. They are almost constantly kept in stables, and fed twice in the day with green meat, of almost every possible variety of vegetation. The collecting this is one of the many agricultural labours constantly performed by women; and it is no inconsiderable feature in the picturesque aspect of the country, that groups of maids and matrons are perpetually seen bearing, with wonderful ease and activity of step, enormous loads of fresh-cut fodder on their heads. I have seen many a pair of bright eyes, and many a dimpled cheek, peeping out sometimes from a bundle of flowery clover, sometimes from a bush formed of the young shoots of forest-trees, and not unfrequently from the thrifty gatherings of every weed, or handful of tufted grass, that grows beside the road. That there is much economy of everything but labour in this, is very evident; and, as far as I was able to judge, the cows prospered marvellously by this regular mode of furnishing their meals in the stall, instead of permitting them to be constantly browsing in the fields. I never met with either bad butter or adulterated milk; and it appeared to me that there was a greater abundance, and freer use of both, than I had been accustomed to see elsewhere.

I rejoiced to find myself, on the 9th of June, in so very Catholic a country; for the ceremonies by which the *Fête-Dieu* was celebrated were really splendid, considering the size of the town. The streets were lined with double rows of young straight-grown fir-trees; every house being charged with the expense of purchasing such, and having them stuck in for the occasion. In the open places of the city, groups of these same slender trees supported wreaths and garlands of flowers, under which the host was carried in a splendid ark.

The Curé, who bore this in his hands, was himself superbly dressed; and at each corner of the canopy, borne above his head, walked a child of four or five years old, in fancy costume, that looked as if it had been arranged by a ballet-master. Three of them had wings; and the fourth, dressed as an infant St. John, would have been a beautiful model for a painter. The procession consisted of all the military in the garrison, a numerous cortège of priests, with their attendants, and the various associated companies of the town. But by far the prettiest part of the spectacle consisted of the double row of little girls, elegantly dressed in white, their heads adorned with wreaths of roses, and long white veils. Above two hundred of these pretty creatures, looking all smiles and gladness, followed the host; and when the procession paused, while the awful symbol was laid on the altar of the different *reposoirs* prepared to receive it, they, as well as the assembled multitude, who followed them, prostrated themselves upon the ground before it. The children all visited the Curé in his sacristy as soon as the ceremony was over, and each received from him a little *cornet* of *bonbons*.

I made many visits during the progress of the procession, with my friend, Mrs. F——, to houses advantageously situated for giving a good view of it. This seemed to be the fashion, for we met large parties at several of them. Some of these houses were extremely handsome and well fitted up.

After all this was over, we went with a party to visit a rustic hotel, at the distance of two miles from Ostend, where a dinner had been bespoken for us. To see the master of this establishment was the chief object of the excursion; and he is, indeed, a very interesting personage. Without education, or advantage of any kind, beyond what his own active intellect and industry supplied, this M. Paret has made himself an excellent naturalist; and has collected a valuable cabinet of curious specimens in various branches of science. In particular, he has many beautifully arranged skeletons of remarkable fish, put together by himself. Of his ability in this branch of art, all those may judge, who saw the skeleton of the whale exhibited in the King's Mews; for the preparation of it was entirely the work of his hands. This whale was thrown upon the beach at Ostend, in 1827, and was purchased, from those who had a right to sell it, for the sum of one thousand francs. The purchaser immediately asked, and obtained, the willing aid of Paret; and by him it was arranged exactly as it was afterwards exhibited. It is painful to add, that for this laborious work the skilful artist is said never to have received any remuneration.

On the 10th of June we proceeded to Bruges, accompanied by the friends whose kindness had contrived to render Ostend extremely agreeable to us, notwithstanding the vexatious accident which had detained us there.

We travelled by one of the pretty packet-boats that navigate the noble canal; choosing this mode of conveyance, both because it was the easiest for my son, and also that we might see a work superior to every thing of the kind in Europe; for in China only, as we were told, can a still more superb canal be seen.

Bruges, and the country round it, is as flat as Ostend, but there is much to see and admire. This fine old city was formerly the capital of Flanders, and remained so till the end of the fifteenth century, being the great Flemish depôt for the commerce of the Hanseatic League. This was the source of its vast wealth; and to this may be traced the relics of former magnificence, which are still to be found there. When the monopoly was transferred to Antwerp, both the splendour and activity of Bruges declined; and I was very gravely assured, that its principal trade at present is in beer and manure.

In fact, there is no appearance of commerce in any part of the city. A walk through the fine old streets, with their high pointed mansions, and richly carved ornaments, is like looking over a portfolio of Prout's best drawings—but there are very few figures in active movement to enliven them. Nevertheless, it was far from being a "dull town to me." There is no quarter that had not some historic record attached to it to excite interest, and gratify curiosity; and it is, therefore, notwithstanding its stillness, well worthy of detaining the traveller for several days. Many of the houses are extremely handsome, and almost all appear comfortable, and scrupulously clean. I never saw a city in which so little appearance of poverty met the eye. I was told that sixteen thousand of the inhabitants (the whole number being thirty-seven thousand) receive aid from public charities. Beggars are certainly seen at the church doors, but the streets exhibit no traces of want, or even of discomfort.

The tower of the Hôtel de Ville is magnificent; and those who take the trouble to climb it are rewarded not only by the panorama of the city, but by so extended and unbroken a map of the country round it, as leaves a more graphic impression of Flemish scenery on the memory than can be obtained by any other means.

The machinery of the chimes, which occupies a room near the top of the tower, is another reward of the labour. It is surprisingly ingenious and elaborate. The enormous barrel, upon which a vast variety of tunes are arranged, is of brass; and is really one of the handsomest instruments I ever saw.

The building containing the public library ought not to remain unseen. Its external form and proportions are singularly elegant. The cathedral church of St. Sauveur is rich, almost to excess, in every species of internal decoration. Carving, gilding, and massive silver, tapestry, painting, and sculpture, are all lavished upon it in profusion; behind the organ, and fronting the western entrance, is a figure of the Almighty, by whose hand I know not; but it is a composition of wonderful power and majesty.

Notre Dame, standing as close to St. Sauveur as St. Margaret's to Westminster Abbey, is large, but very inferior in splendour to its magnificent neighbour. It has the honour, however, of containing the bones of Charles the Bold, and his daughter Mary, the wife of Maximilian. Their tombs of touchstone, superbly decorated, are most costly monumental structures, and are carefully enclosed in wooden cases, removed only on the payment of a fee. This church possesses, also, a simple and very graceful group of the Virgin and Child, said to be by Michael Angelo.

I dare not rehearse all that I saw at Bruges which appeared to me worthy of attention; for the catalogue would be too long for any to read with patience, unless they were about to set off at the instant to visit this museum of antiquities.

The friends who so kindly accompanied us from Ostend introduced us to many of their Bruges acquaintance, which certainly increased the pleasure of our stay in no trifling degree. Among these I may take the liberty of naming one, who is already too well known to the public to make my doing so impertinent. M. Moke, the author of Hermann, is so enthusiastic in his love and admiration of Bruges, and so learnedly familiar with its history, as to make him an invaluable companion among its venerable archives, and mouldering grandeur. It may, perhaps, be partly owing to my having listened to its records from so eloquent an historian, and from having the splendid relics of its brighter days pointed out to me with equal taste and feeling, that I remember this old city with more of interest and admiration than is usually bestowed upon it.

Bruges is often passed almost unnoticed by travellers, whose ultimate object is the Rhine or Switzerland; and while their imaginations are flying forward to rocks and mountains, they scorn the cities of the plain, which lead to them. I strongly recommend all travellers through Belgium to devote at least three days to making themselves well acquainted with the interesting antiquities of Bruges. If they have the good fortune to be introduced to the society of the place, they will be willing to stay much longer.

By what I saw and heard, evening parties are frequent, and very agreeable; though not splendid or ostentatious in any way. We passed one very pleasant evening at the house of M. Moke. The party was small, but so agreeable as to make me think with something like vexation of the enormous throngs, which jostle each other from house to house through a midsummer evening in London. We had singing, that might have made Pasta herself look about her (but this was from an English-woman); and then we fell into some of those playful exercises of wit and fancy for which the French language is so admirably adapted. As I listened to hit after hit, in this trial of wordy skill, I thought that those, who try the same pastime in England, would do well to adopt the language too. It would not only render their *bons-mots* more piquant, but familiarize them with the use of a tongue, which will carry them farther over Europe than any other. It may be childish, perhaps, to indulge in such a sport, and still more childish to record it; but, nevertheless, I own to having been very much amused.—Every one's faculties were brought into play.

"From every head
A lambent flame (of wit) arose, which gently spread
Around the brows and on the fancy fed."

When we had laughed till we were weary, we were refreshed by wine, cakes, and the finest fruit of the season; and so ended the *soirée*.

The old paintings in the hospital of St. John are among the things that must be seen at Bruges. In the chapel they show a coffer, said to contain a bone of St. Ursula, the exterior case of which is painted on panel by Hemling, with a delicacy of finish that is perfectly astonishing. The subject is the dismal history of the arrival of her eleven thousand virgins at Cologne; and the number of figures introduced defies any reasonable hope of graceful composition; but in the year 1579 this was a branch of the art not well understood; and no deficiency in it could have lowered the estimation in which this gem must have been held. It is still "a thing to wonder at;" but in the sixteenth century it might almost have been deemed miraculous.

On leaving the chapel, I accepted the invitation of a Catholic lady, to accompany her round the female wards of the hospital. The rest of the party declined joining us, from a fear of encountering disagreeable objects; but they were wrong. The pain, which the sight, or even the idea of human suffering must ever occasion, was a thousand times overbalanced by the pleasure of witnessing the tender care, the sedulous attention, the effective usefulness of those heavenly-minded beings, *Les Sœurs de la Charité.* It is they who are the only nurses in this large establishment. Unpaid, uncontrolled by any, they give their lives to comfort and help those, who would find neither comfort nor help without them.

I remember being told, by a lively young woman in America, who was sadly tormented by her "helps," that her only idea of heaven was a place full of servants. With a little variation I could almost echo her phrase, and say, that my idea of heaven was a place filled with Sisters of Charity.

Perhaps I shall hear that I am turned Catholic, if I confess that the treasured symbols of that demonstrative faith, which I there saw so fondly cherished in the hour of suffering and of death, touched my heart more than it offended my orthodoxy. The dying eye, expending its last beam in a look of confiding hope at the image of the Redeemer, at that moment suggested no idea of superstition.

One of the curiosities of Bruges, that I will not omit to mention, though I confess I have great doubts of the veracity of the legend on which its chief interest rests, is the little building called the Jerusalem Chapel. It is said to have been built by a burgomaster of the city, most accurately on the model of the Holy Sepulchre at Jerusalem. This story, which was pointed out to me in a very ancient volume of the city library, states that the pious founder of the chapel himself made three pilgrimages to Jerusalem, to ascertain some doubtful points in the architecture; but, at last, the vow he had registered to complete a faithful copy was declared to be fully accomplished; and this memorial of his piety is preserved with all the care which a building, bearing such a form, might be expected to meet in one of the most deeply Catholic cities left on the earth. It is a singular little edifice; and those who love things out of the common way will think it worth visiting.

There is a very grotesque group, and well worth looking at, in alto relievo, over the door of a brewhouse; but I cannot instruct any traveller where to find it, as I totally forget the name of the street. It represents, in a very Catholic manner, the process of brewing. There are several figures employed in mashing, and cooling, and putting the beer into casks, while winged seraphs are seen tasting it; and the Virgin Mary, with the infant Jesus in her arms, sits apart to superintend the whole.

At Bruges, and, as we afterwards found, in many other Flemish towns, they have a weekly market for the sale of every kind of second-hand goods, which is called *le Marché au Vendredi*. This is well worth seeing. It is always held in some open place of the town, and offers a most singular spectacle. Beds and pictures, kettles and old clothes, books and fire-irons, and thousands of other heterogeneous articles, are all displayed together in most orderly confusion. Where this weekly display of worn-out trash can come from is puzzling; but it is still more so, to imagine how so many persons of various ranks, and always with some highly respectable among them, can be found to fancy every seventh day that they have need of such trumpery; yet I never saw a Marché au Vendredi that was not thronged.

Our accommodations at the Hôtel de Commerce were excellent. We dined twice, during our stay, at the table d'hôte, where a very good dinner is very neatly served for two francs a head. When we dined in our own apartments, the expense was about double; but we might then have fancied ourselves at one of the best restaurants in Paris.

CHAPTER II.

Ghent — Antiquities — St. Bavon — The University— Schamp's Collection—Bull Fight—Espions—Beguinage—St. Michael's—Antwerp—Spanish Air—Effects of the Siege.

OUR Ostend friends still accompanied us when we left Bruges for Ghent. The distance is about twenty-seven English miles. Here again we found ourselves surrounded by buildings of the most picturesque form and colour; with the additional novelty of numerous canals cutting through the town in all directions, and connecting the rivers Scheldt and Lys.

Volumes might be fairly and worthily filled by mere catalogues of the antiquities which an industrious amateur might find in these glorious old Flemish towns. No story of the days that are gone, though we have had some which seemed to bring past ages before us by an enchanter's wand, can throw so forcible a light on that portion of history which relates to the period of Flemish splendour, as the sight of these laboured relics themselves. We read, in most speaking hieroglyphics, through every street, a commentary on the manners, customs, wealth, and taste of this interesting country.

The vast warerooms reaching up to the very pinnacle of the steep and pointed gable that finishes the richly-ornamented mansion, show that the wealthy merchant lived splendidly under the same roof which sheltered his wares; while the large door-way that opens from more than one of the upper stories, and not seldom the traces of a crane beside it, prove that the portly dames who sat in the "look-out," had no objection to seeing the merchandise, on which their style and state depended, hoisted and lowered before their windows. Then rises, close beside the merchant's house, the proud tower which marks the dwelling of a noble. None else were permitted to erect this symbol of power and dignity.

At one point is seen the costly stadt-house, ornamented with carving without and painting within, of a finish which must have been paid by most unsparing expenditure of civic gold. At another rises a magnificent church, so grand in its conception, so gorgeous in its decoration, and so abounding in riches of every kind, as to tell loudly of the wealth of those by whom its pillared aisles were reared, and its accumulated treasures deposited.

In short, it appeared to me that, instead of treating Flanders merely as a high road to the Rhine, all who have time, and feel pleasure in examining objects, the ideas of which have been long familiar to them, should pause long, and study carefully, every city on the route.

Two young students of the University assisted our kind companions in showing all that was most interesting in Ghent. And here, as at Bruges, the variety of objects makes it difficult to rehearse what we saw. The magnificent cathedral of St. Bavon was the first thing visited. This church is more than ordinarily interesting in every way. It is of great antiquity, and full of interesting memorials relative to the history of the city, and indicative of its former importance. There are several inscriptions in the choir, which commemorate the institution of the order of the Golden Fleece, by Philip the Good; and the different chapters of the order which have been held in the church. The date of the first is 1440. The length and height of the aisles are magnificent; and the choir a perfect museum of splendid decorations. In a chapel to the north of the high altar is a fine picture by Rubens, painted for the place where it hangs. It represents St. Bavon, in the act of renouncing the things of this world, and distributing his wealth to the poor. The whole composition is very fine; and a group in the foreground, of a woman on her knees, with two children, most lovely.

The pulpit of this church is considered to be one of the richest in Flanders, both in style and execution. It is a mixture of carved wood and white marble, having many parts very richly gilt. Notwithstanding all the splendour of this superb cathedral, the portion of it which gave me most pleasure was the subterranean church beneath. There is something so solemn in its sombre vastness, and so venerable in its untouched antiquity, that I returned to its dark aisles more than once; and examined the naked strength and capricious irregularity of the structure with more interest, and a more awakened imagination, than all the magnificence above had excited.

In fact, one feels in every fine old church, however remote its date, and unquestioned its antiquity, that every age which has passed over it has changed its aspect, as much as it has increased its splendour. But when standing among the sturdy pillars of the subterranean St. Bavon, the thousand years that have rolled by, since its roughly-hewn stones were piled together, seem to vanish; and you see at a glance how the Christians of 800 wrought.

I remember feeling something of the same effect in the underground church at Canterbury; but it is by no means equal in any way to that of Ghent. Almost all the principal churches in Catholic towns are called cathedrals, though many of them have neither bishop nor chapter. St. Bavon's, however, is really such; and I had the great delight of hearing and seeing a Sunday high mass performed there. The music was very fine; many stringed instruments adding their clear and thrilling notes to those of the organ. The bishop himself, and a very large assemblage of the clergy of the cathedral, assisted at the ceremony; and, altogether, the service was performed with a degree of dignity and solemn stateliness, which no difference of faith could prevent my feeling to be deeply and religiously impressive.

The University of Ghent is a very handsome building, erected by the king of Holland. The portico is Grecian, and of noble dimensions; and the circular hall, for the examination of the students, peculiarly elegant;—but the name of William of Holland is effaced from the inscription on the portico; and a sheet of white paper covers his coat of arms, which are embroidered on the drapery on one side of this graceful amphitheatre. It was very evident, by the tone in which one or two young men, who had joined us, spoke of this eclipse, that it was considered as throwing a shade over the glory of Ghent. In truth, king William has been a most munificent patron to the town; and it can surprise no one that his name should still be pronounced there with affection and regret.

The collection of objects in natural history appears to be admirably arranged; and the whole establishment is one that would do honour to any country.

In the church of St. Michael is an excellent picture by Vandyke, but in very bad condition. The Academy of Painting contains good and sufficient rooms for any institution of the kind; but the collection of pictures is most lamentably French. It is grievous, in a country teeming with the works of Vandyke and Rubens, to see the wretched school of David prevailing so generally among the young artists. One fine well-lighted room is entirely occupied by pictures to which the annual prizes have been awarded for the last twenty years. They are all of them strictly after the French school. One of our spring fashions in London is to declare unanimously every year, that "the Exhibition at Somerset-house is very so so;"—"very little worth looking at;" and the like. I wish all our critics would pass a few months on the continent, expressly for the purpose of making themselves well acquainted with its modern pictures. I think they would return much less dissatisfied with our own.

The Baron von Schamp's collection is too well known to make the mention of it useful to English travellers; but it is difficult not to indulge in the pleasure of dwelling on the recollection of such a treat. The two full-length portraits of Vandyke —Rembrandt's portrait of himself—and, above all else, the "Annunciation" of Corregio, will, I hope and believe, never pass from my memory. To insure this, as much as my time at Ghent permitted, I visited the collection twice, remaining there two or three hours each time; and I do not recollect ever enjoying pictures more completely. There is just as much attendance on the part of the person who shows them as is necessary, and no more—no throng of company to step between you and the object of your contemplation; and no yawning, weary servant to hasten the delightful lounge to its close. I never saw any painting that I so much coveted for our national gallery, as the little picture of Corregio above named. In taste, feeling, composition, and execution, it is exactly what I should wish to place for ever before the eyes of our students. The composition consists of a single figure. No visible angel divides the attention with this sweet portraiture of the Virgin. Mary is holding a small volume in her hand, which one feels certain is the Bible; she has closed the book, but her thumb is between the leaves, at the passage which has caused her to pause in meditation. Her eyes are raised to heaven with an expression of such deep and earnest devotion, as instantly to suggest the idea of her having just read the words of Isaiah, "a virgin shall conceive and bear a son;" and of her feeling that she, even she, might be the chosen one. A ray from heaven falls upon her uplifted face, and cold must be the heart, and dead the fancy, that does not feel the holy beauty of the idea.

If one of the very few showers which annoyed us during the summer had not chanced to fall at Ghent on the evening of the 16th of June, I should have been present at a bull-fight, notwithstanding the disgust which the idea of such a spectacle suggested. The advertisement made me expect to witness something in the true Spanish style, where men were the combatants instead of dogs. This horror, as we were assured, is sanctioned by the Belgic laws; and does not seem to be considered either as degrading to the men, or cruel to the beasts engaged in it. Though I would willingly have enabled myself to give some account of an amusement so truly foreign, I was not very sorry, at the moment, to escape it; yet, by what I afterwards heard, there is more trick than daring in the matador, who however stops short of deserving the title; and the scene in the arena has about as much resemblance to the awful bull-fights of old, as the *simayrees* between Miss Jacko, and those who acted with her, to the chances of a genuine elephant hunt.

The fashion of having "espions" at the windows, though we remarked it in every city through which we passed, is more than usually prevalent at Ghent. Notwithstanding its being evidently so very common a contrivance, it was quite new to me; and as it is possible it may be equally so to others, I mention it as being certainly connected with national manners. By means of mirrors placed on the outside of the drawing-room windows, those who sit within are enabled to see all that passes without; and yet never be guilty of the indecorum of appearing at the window. As these machines are arranged with hinges, which admit every variety of position, they are not unfrequently so placed as to present to the passer-by the reflection of a pretty face, while the person to whom it belongs is safely ensconced within. The first time I saw one of these contrivances, my attention was drawn to it by the vision of a young bright-looking countenance peeping at me from amidst a profusion of ringlets; and as it was surrounded by a square frame, I thought, at the first glance, that it was a picture hung out at the window to show that portraits done in the same style were to be seen within. A few steps in advance showed me who the artist was.

There are still several convents left in Flanders; and we frequently saw, both at Bruges and Ghent, Beguine sisters in the streets and markets. At the latter place, the Beguinage is a very handsome establishment. We attended the *salut* in their chapel, and saw seven hundred of them at their devotions. The effect of this large assemblage of kneeling nuns was very beautiful. Many were in the bloom of youth, and the costume is far from unbecoming. When the service ended, they all rose, and many drew near the altar to perform some little additional act of devotion, or of penitence, on the steps of it. As each prepared to depart, she took off her veil, which is of delicate white linen, and, folding it up, placed it flat upon the top of her head; producing exactly the effect of the square head-dress, with which we are so familiar in Italian pictures.

The knowledge that these secluded women might be absolved from their vows, if they became weary of the peaceful but monotonous life they enjoin, prevented the spectacle from exciting in us any painful feeling of regret for the sacrifice they had made of the joys, the hopes, and affections of the world. It is very rarely however, as we were assured from many quarters, that any are found who wish to take advantage of this. They live with great comfort, their moderate incomes producing, when thrown together, a revenue more than equal to their expenses. The whole establishment, with its church, is enclosed within walls, which may, however, be freely entered at all hours of the day. They are not lodged in one large building, as is usual in other convents, but have quite a little town within their walls, each house of which is inhabited by one or more sisters and their servants. These houses have most of them the names of the inhabitants on a plate over the door, as "Sister Bertha," "Sister Gertrude;" and on others we read "Sainte Adelaide," "Sainte Lucia," and so on. Many ladies of good families reside among them, and we saw more than one handsome carriage at their doors. I believe they are chosen as godmothers for half the population; and altogether seem, as far as I could judge, to be of more consequence, each in her own circle, than they would have been, had they retained their situations as individual single women, instead of becoming members of a large community.

Mr. H. being desirous of taking a sketch from a nun in full costume, expressed the wish to a lady to whom he had been introduced. She was a Catholic, and having some friend or relation in a convent of Ste. Therese, kindly undertook to procure him the opportunity he wished. He accompanied her to the gates, which were opened by an aged sister, to whom Madame L—— explained the motive of her visit, requesting to see sister ——, naming a junior member of the community.

"Should not I serve the purpose as well?" inquired the venerable nun.

Mr. H. looked dismayed; Madame L. hesitated.

"We all wear the same habit;" persisted the old woman.

But a whispered word of entreaty from the disappointed artist induced Madame L. to persevere in her request; and they were ushered into a parlour, where a very pretty young woman soon appeared. Mr. H. immediately drew out his sketch-book.

"I hope it is for the honour of the good cause?" said the young nun.

Madame L. assured her that she might be certain of it; and a very pretty drawing was made.

On the 17th of June we left Ghent for Antwerp; and again had the satisfaction of prevailing on our friends from Ostend to prolong their excursion for a few days. Though the roads through Flanders have no beauty of scenery to recommend them, they are by no means without interest, especially in the summer. The country is a perfect garden; every inch is cultivated; and the variety of crops standing together without the interval of hedges, or division of any kind, I think, enhances the idea of their profuse abundance. It was, however, only when they began reaping their abundant harvest, that we became fully aware of the prodigious fertility of the soil. It seemed like cutting a slice out of a solid cake. The simile is not elegant, perhaps, but no other image suggests itself.

Between Ghent and Antwerp we passed through the little town of St. Nicholas, said to be the largest flax market in the world. It is better to travel through its vicinity during the early summer, than the early autumn; for from the time the delicate flax crop ceases to wave its slight blue bells in the fields, to that in which it assumes the dainty form of lace or cambric thread, it perfectly poisons the air.

The direct carriage-road from Ghent to Antwerp is by the Tête de Flandre; but owing to the inundation, occasioned by cutting the dikes during the bombardment of the town, we were obliged to leave the road, and embark on the Scheldt. It is a noble river, as all the world knows; but at this time the objects visible from it, on approaching Antwerp, are more than usually interesting. The ruined citadel, the dilapidated depôts, and the inundated plain, all spoke of recent war and havoc. But as we advanced, our eyes rose from earth to heaven, as the beautiful spire of the cathedral became visible. It is nowhere seen to greater advantage, in respect to its light and graceful proportions, than from the river: but the ornaments are too intricate and delicate to show themselves well at any great distance; and till you are near enough to distinguish these, I think the general effect would be better were the outline more simple.

We took up our quarters at the *grand Hotel St. Antoine,* from the windows of which this elegant spire may be studied to great advantage. The circumstance that most forcibly struck me, in my first walk through Antwerp, was the Spanish air of the women. We had remarked something of this, both at Bruges and Ghent, but by no means in so great a degree. At Antwerp the mantilla is universal among the women. The higher classes indeed there, as everywhere else, are as nearly Parisian in appearance as they can contrive to be; but many among the wealthy bourgeoisie wear this graceful drapery of costly materials, and arranged with great care and elegance. In many instances the cloak is changed for an ample veil of rich black silk, that completely envelops the head and shoulders. In both dresses the face is concealed in a considerable degree; and when in the act of devotion, no part of the countenance is permitted to be visible. The long black rows of veiled heads, which we constantly saw in the churches, often made me fancy myself surrounded by nuns.

Nor is it in the dress alone that the Flemish

citizens show traces of their Spanish ancestors. We remarked many beautiful women, who, both in feature and complexion, gave indication of southern forefathers. Yet, if I mistake not, it was under Philip the Second that Flanders revolted from Spain. One should imagine that years enough had passed over them to obliterate all this; but, most assuredly, the fact is otherwise. The deep catholicism too, so infinitely beyond that of any neighbouring people, cannot, I think, be so reasonably traced to any other source.

Here again, as in the other cities we had passed through, we enjoyed that peculiar and vivid species of pleasure which results from encountering, at every step, some record of long-past events, made familiar to us by history, and the confirmation or destruction of the various fanciful minutiæ with which imagination had connected them. I hardly think that Rome itself can furnish such an incessant succession of pictures as Belgium. I do not mean on panel or canvass, but in all the startling, powerful force of reality. The picturesque outlines of the buildings, their rich and harmonious colouring, together with the costume of every group you meet, arrange themselves into compositions of wonderful grace and interest.

The recent siege furnished but too many additions to these. I had never seen with my own eyes the horrors produced by war, till I visited Antwerp; and I shuddered at remembering, while I looked on the desolation it had left, how lightly I had heard its short and unimportant history mentioned. The crumbling ruins of many public buildings, and the dismal stillness of the dismantled warehouses, are sad spectacles; but these are gay, compared to the fearful waste of waters that lie upon the ruined hopes of the poor peasantry. I had so lately been occupied in wondering at the teeming plenty of the land, that this miserable contrast came upon me with double horror. Seven prosperous villages have been swept away by the flood produced by opening the dikes. Their steeples alone remain above the water to show that they have been.

It is remarkable that, notwithstanding the excessive suffering which this must have produced, no feeling of enmity is expressed by the inhabitants against General Chassé. On the contrary, his conduct is declared to have been as humane and considerate towards the town, as the nature of the task enjoined him would permit; and, in proof of this, a handsome piece of plate has been subscribed for, and presented to him by the citizens, as a memorial of their gratitude. In fact, I believe that no people engaged in the painful labour of repairing the devastation of a siege, ever looked upon the enemy who carried it on with so gentle and forgiving an eye as the worthy inhabitants of Antwerp. They certainly have not forgotten old attachments in recent disunion.

Chapter III.

Antwerp—Notre Dame—Rubens—Academy—Vandyke—Calvary—Passports—Voitures—Arrival at Brussels—Belgian Politics—M. Alexander Rodenbach—Chamber of Representatives—Duel—Society—Palace of the Prince of Orange—Mint—MM. Vandermaelen—M. Robyns—Du Bos—Theatre—St. Gudule—Old Town—Louvain— Tervueren—Dilapidations—Tree of Liberty.

Though I am quite determined not to omit the mention of any object which particularly interested me, merely because it has often been mentioned before, yet I fear I may not venture to indulge in speaking much at length of the churches of Belgium. There is something dangerously beguiling in the subject. It is so easy to recall to one's self where and how the effect produced by each noble pile differed or agreed. The rich windows here, the graceful arches there; the stupendous roof of one, and the wondrous aisles of another; all come so readily back to one's own eye, and are so difficult to set before the eyes of another, that, I believe, the safest way will be to pass my pen through all notes respecting them, written in the moment of enthusiasm.

But for this precaution, I might be tempted to transcribe many a futile page, descriptive of the church of Notre Dame at Antwerp. It is indeed a noble edifice; and one might almost be excused for losing one's self, for awhile, amid the pillared labyrinths of its seven aisles. The acknowledged chef-d'œuvre of Rubens hangs in this church. The Descent from the Cross is, indeed, a powerful picture; and exhibits most splendidly all the various species of excellence for which the pencil of Rubens is celebrated; yet it did not quite realize the expectations I had formed of it. The attitude of St. John has more of the graceful posture-master, than of the desolate disciple in it; and the gorgeous colouring of the picture, richly harmonious as it is, seems more in accordance with the taste of the artist, than with the tone of the scene.

I had the courage to mount the lofty steeple and was rewarded by having Bergen-op-Zoom,

Flushing, Breda, Ghent, and Mechlin pointed out as visible specks in the distance. Though quite calm below, the wind was tremendous at the elevation to which we had climbed, but I battled it stoutly for half an hour. From this height the devastations of the siege may be fully traced in every direction; and the sight is sad enough.

On the following day we crossed the Scheldt, to see the works by which the Belgians are endeavouring to repair the breach in the dike. A thousand workmen are employed upon it; but they proceed very slowly, as the tide sometimes destroys in a night the labour of many days.

The Academy contains a large collection of pictures, and many of them are of first-rate excellence. Among these is one by Vandyke, which if placed beside the Rubens of Notre Dame, would exemplify perfectly what it is that I found, or fancied, wanting in that master-piece. The scene and the persons are the same; the time somewhat later. The body of Jesus is laid on the lap of his mother; St. John is placed near her, holding one of the Saviour's hands; and the Magdalen stands quietly apart, looking with tearful eyes at the group. The agony of the mother is the most speaking passion I ever saw upon canvass; and the sober tone of the whole picture is in beautiful accordance with the awful hour.

We made many attempts to see the citadel, having flattered ourselves that an application from a diplomatic friend, who was with us, must meet a favourable answer; but in this we were disappointed. The impediments thrown in our way seemed frivolous and vexatious in no common degree. Sometimes our applications were answered by words of hope and civility; but delay was always the sequel; till at last we gave up the attempt rather in disgust than despair.

There is a singular monkish relic at Antwerp, less known and visited than, I think, its elaborate piety deserves. This is a representation of Calvary at the ancient convent of the Dominicans. It is reared with an almost grotesque boldness of design against the church of St. Paul's, which formerly made part of the convent. This church forms one side of an interior court, into which the convent windows look; and against it, mounting to the very top of the building, is the extraordinary collection of statues and of rocks, which they call Mount Calvary. There are above sixty figures as large as life. I believe the whole to be in stone; but the effect very nearly approaches that of marble; and some of the groups have a very graceful and imposing outline. The entire area of the court is converted into a sort of Pantheon of saints, statues of half the calendar being stuck about in all directions.

The Holy Sepulchre is at the foot of the mount; and is at present guarded by an old woman, who for two sous opens the grated door, and permits you to enter. Nothing can be more lamentably ludicrous than this part of the show. The figure of the Saviour is dressed in a drapery of tawdry muslin and lace; and a dingy little lamp burns at its feet.

Our last hours at Antwerp were rendered extremely tedious and unprofitable by the difficulty of getting our passports returned to us. The first annoyance was being told, when we sent a commissioner for them, that they would not be given to him, but that we must go ourselves. We did so; but found the office shut. We were assured, however, by many who were standing near, that the person whose duty it was to examine them would be there in a few minutes. We departed, and returned in half an hour, but the door was still closed. Again we departed and again returned; but still the functionary was not in his place. Nearly half our last day at Antwerp was spent thus; and when at last we succeeded in finding the man of office, and informed him of the inconvenience to which we had been put by his absence, the " brave Belge " put himself into a very exceeding rage; and declared that if another word of the kind were spoken, we should not have our passports till the next day, adding, with much emphasis, " Je crois bien qu'un fonctionaire, quel qu'il soit, vaut au moins autant que le premier venu."

An English gentleman, who accompanied us to the office, advised him *not to refuse our passports;* and after a blustering look or two at each of us, he condescended to execute the duty with which he was entrusted.

Soon after this troublesome business was settled, we took leave, with much regret, of the friends who had accompanied us thus far on our journey; and departed for Brussels in the diligence at a late hour in the evening. We afterwards found ample reason to repent this arrangement; for we had no subsequent opportunity of seeing the beautiful church at Mechlin; and the moonlight just showed enough of its fine old tower, as we passed it, to make us exceedingly regret not seeing more.

And here, for the benefit of such of my readers as may chance to travel in the same humble style as myself, I may observe, that whenever the travelling party exceeds two, the diligence is a dearer mode of conveyance than a voiture with one pair of horses. If, indeed, speed be an important point, the traveller must post with four horses, for in no other way can he attain it. But a good voiturier will take you nearly, if not quite, as fast as the diligence: and in this mode you are not only master of your own time of setting out and arriving, but are not exposed to the vexation of being whirled past objects that you are longing to gaze upon. In this respect, indeed, posting is very nearly as bad as the diligence, for, once started upon a stage, it would be difficult to make a post-boy pause, *en route,* for your pleasure, even if St. Peter's itself rose up to be looked at midway.

I know few things more dismal than arriving in a city before its population are awake. This was our fate at Brussels; and though we immediately mounted from the narrow streets of the old town to the bright and splendid region of the new, it was some hours before we were sufficiently recovered from our weariness and discomfort to enjoy thoroughly the gay aspect of the place. Before the morning was half over, however, we were established in pleasant apartments at the *hôtel garni* on the Boulevard, and quite ready to enjoy all the agreeable varieties of one of the prettiest little capitals in Europe.

Every one told us that Brussels was no longer the delightful city to dwell in that it had been before the revolution—that many families, both native and foreign, had forsaken it—and that both pleasure and business went on sluggishly. This, I dare say, may be very true; and yet Brussels is still delightful.

The park, and the handsome streets round it, the Place-Royale, the beautiful boulevard, the public buildings, and the noble palaces, show themselves better, and altogether produce a more brilliant *coup-d'œil* than any place I have seen.

Though we had made no very long abode in Belgium, we had not passed through it without having heard much that was interesting as to its political position; and I felt considerable curiosity to hear the same subject discussed in its capital, and to learn, by entering the Chamber of Representatives, what the tone of debate might be in a country so singularly situated.

The whole of the British nation must, I think, ever feel a deep and affectionate interest for the amiable prince who has been induced to accept the throne of Belgium. It is impossible to forget how near he has been to England; and it should be at least equally so, not to remember how perfectly free from reproach has been the tenor of his remarkable life. With these feelings of respect and attachment to King Leopold, it is impossible not to lament his being placed in the situation he now holds. Everything I heard of him personally, and I conversed with those who had the best means of knowing him well, convinced me that he deserves to rule over a people more attached to his dynasty than the late subjects of the King of Holland are ever likely to be.

No one, I believe, could pass a month in Belgium, and converse as freely with people of all parties as I did, without becoming aware that the King of Holland still reigns in the hearts of the majority; and that any person, however illustrious, who had become the instrument of the factious demagogues employed to dismember his kingdom, could have little chance of retaining his station were the genuine wishes of the Belgians themselves alone consulted. That abuses had crept into King William's government—that vexatious imposts, hardly worth contending for, had been unwisely persisted in—and that some personal jealousies existed between the Dutch and the Belgians, may be very true: but these things were neither sufficient to justify revolution, nor to render the result of it permanent. That such are now the reflections of many of those who were led away by popular tumult, I truly believe; and the number of these is more likely to increase than diminish.

No political revolution can take place without putting men's minds into a species of fever, very unfit for sane and temperate reasoning. The state which follows is often one of quiescence and languor; but when this passes off, they find, perhaps, that some useful lessons may have been learnt, even during their delirium. Nevertheless, a very natural fear of new disturbances may long keep even a powerful majority passive.

If I may believe the representations which reached me from many quarters, no country was ever revolutionized by a feeling so little general as that which severed Belgium from Holland. The deed was done at Brussels; and many of the most effective agents in it were as alien to the country as hostile to the King. That some honest men were led to believe that they should serve their country by changing its government, there can be no doubt; but even these must now feel something not unlike remorse, when they see how very little of real independence they have obtained for her.

Without entering into any discussion respecting the new institutions acquired by Belgium under the recent constitution, or inquiring whether they be or be not politically wiser than some which have been discarded, I believe I shall run no great risk of being contradicted if I say, that the spirit and intelligence of the general mass of the population do in no degree harmonize and accord with them. Nothing can present a stranger anomaly in human affairs, than the sight of a nation, deeply and severely Catholic, attempting to ape the chartered libertinism of political thinking, which a few noisy and discontented persons are endeavouring to teach them. The law which authorizes unrestrained license of tongue and pen, both public and private, on all subjects, whether political or religious, accords ill with the principles of a people whose religion commands them to bring their thoughts, words, and deeds before the tribunal of their priests.

With one hand thus unresistingly shackled, and a club or a dagger put by law into the other, the Belgian citizen can hardly be expected to present himself to the world under an aspect either of dignity or usefulness.

We did not wait long ere we obtained admission to the Chamber of Representatives; and, in consequence of an introduction from an acquaintance I made at Bruges, we were accompanied thither by a very charming person, the wife and sister-in-law of two gentlemen highly distinguished as among the most influential orators of the Lower Chamber. It was impossible to make the acquaintance of the MM. Rodenbach without feeling sincere admiration for the talents of both. This tribute of praise I can hardly hope will be acceptable to these distinguished men from an obscure individual, whom not even their eloquence could teach to think as they do in the science to which they have devoted themselves: nevertheless I offer it in all sincerity, and shall certainly not easily forget the amiable reception they accorded me. M. Alexandre Rodenbach is one of the most interesting persons I have ever met. He is totally blind; and the stillness which this misfortune gives to his outward aspect is so forcibly contrasted with the brilliant vivacity of the spirit within, as to make the effect of his animated language almost electric. His work, entitled ' Coup-d'œil d'un Aveugle sur les Sourds-muets,' would have been deeply interesting from any hand, but from his it is very peculiarly so; and both in this little volume, and in his ' Lettre sur les Aveugles, faisant Suite à celle de Diderot,' there is a tone of such true and amiable philosophy, as to create no common degree of kindness towards their author. In short, if we can but amicably agree to differ in politics, there are few people with whom I should be more happy to renew acquaintance than M. Alexandre Rodenbach.

We heard some sharp debating in the Chamber, and the Belgian Ministry could hardly have been more vehemently assailed, had they been placed in their stations by King William himself.

There is a vivacity of indignation about all M. Dumortier utters, that must constantly insure attention. I have often observed that the majority of people like to listen to violent scolding, provided it be not addressed to themselves; and as M. Dumortier employs all his eloquence in pointing out the exceeding wickedness of the Ministers, the rest of the Chamber appear to hear him with great satisfaction.

M. Gendebien is another orator to whom every eye is turned when he rises to speak; but I fancied more than once that his lively sallies produced a greater inclination to smile than to frown in those he attacked. In this, however, I presume I was mistaken, for some of his words were so seriously received, that they produced a duel, before we left Brussels, between himself and M. Rogier, the Minister of the Interior.

Affairs of this kind are so frequent among the ardent spirits of this young government, that it has become a daily exercise among the gentlemen to fire with pistols at a mark; and M. Gendebein is said to have reached such a pitch of dexterity, as to be able to bring down a bee upon the wing with the nicest certainty. In consideration of such peculiar skill, the seconds in this affair placed the combatants at the unusual distance of thirty-six paces; but the Opposition deputy sustained his reputation, and wounded his official enemy in the mouth.

We were dining with Prince Auguste d'Aremberg*, the day after the meeting took place, and it naturally became the topic of conversation at table. "Gendebein always hits where he aims," said the lively Prince; "he wanted to stop Rogier's tongue, and he therefore sent a shot through his mouth."

I believe it is the fashion at Brussels, either after killing or wounding an adversary, to retire for a few days, for I missed M. Gendebien from the Chamber after this rencontre; and upon another occasion of the kind, which unhappily had a fatal termination, I learnt that *going out of town* for a short time was the only result. I have seldom felt more shocked and astonished than I did, on learning that a young Belgian officer, with whom we dined in company, and whose light and amiable

* This amiable nobleman died within three months after we left Brussels. His loss will be deeply felt in the circle in which he lived, and of which, notwithstanding his great age, he was the ornament and delight.

gaiety of manner had particularly struck me, had the day before killed a gentleman in a duel, for some political difference of opinion. I did not know of this till the morning his unfortunate victim was buried, and then I recollected a few words, which had been addressed to him at table, evidently alluding to the circumstance.

"I thought, * * * *, you were going out of town?" said a whiskered militaire, addressing him.

"Yes; I shall take myself off to-morrow, for a couple of days," he replied.

The *morrow* was the day fixed for the funeral.

I am persuaded that neither the tumult, the ruin, nor even the massacre, produced by a political revolution, are its worst features. It shakes social order to the very centre—puts all moral feeling out of joint—and makes virtue herself turn giddy. There are many honest men who would shudder at their own theories, could they see them stripped of the mystifications with which a sort of patriotic slang has veiled them. But it is a hard fate for those who are both honest and clear-sighted too, to witness all the elements of social life thrown into confusion—the sturdy materials that nature formed to be the base of the pyramid hoisted, in defiance of all philosophy, to the top, while the polished work that crowned it is thrown to the earth, and trampled in the dust.

Some arrangements after this fashion are the inevitable consequence of every great political commotion; and it requires no great depth of scrutiny to discover symptoms of the kind at Brussels. The consequence of this has been the breaking up, in a great degree, of the delightful circle of society for which it used to be celebrated. Many of the noblesse have altogether withdrawn themselves; and few of those who remain are as accessible as formerly. We were assured by a Russian officer, that all the gaiety now to be found at Brussels must be sought in the mansions of the English; and that, without this resource, no one, who had a choice, would continue to make that city his residence. This assurance might possibly have been occasioned by the politeness of the speaker towards the party addressed; but, as I repeatedly heard the same statement from the Belgians themselves, I am inclined to believe it is the fact.

We had the good fortune, however, to make the acquaintance of many agreeable people during our short stay; and had not the object of our excursion been to wander much farther, I should have well liked to have passed a month or two at Brussels. As it was, we could allow ourselves but one short fortnight; but we made the most of it, and regularly spent our mornings in seeing sights, and our evenings in very agreeable society. We had the pleasure of dining with the British Minister, whose elegant hospitality and pleasing manners must contribute, in no trifling degree, to render a residence at Brussels agreeable.

The Palace of the Prince of Orange is not only the first object of admiration in the capital of Belgium; but would, I presume, be considered in every part of the world as a finished model of a splendid palace. It is not large; but, I think, it may be called perfect in magnificence and in taste: at least, I can imagine nothing superior to the superb elegance of the furniture and decorations. The date of its completion is 1828, when it was immediately inhabited by the Prince and Princess.

It is certainly not easy to conceive a more striking

occasion for meditation on the uncertainty of human affairs, than the sight of this gorgeous, yet desolate palace suggests. In 1828, the princely founder took assured possession of its marble halls—and in 1830 they know him no longer!

Every thing within the palace is kept in the most perfect order. The visitors, who throng to see it, walk over the inlaid floors in list shoes, which are furnished by the guide, who watches every individual with jealous attention, lest the envelope should slip aside, and vulgar shoe-leather approach the beautiful *parquet*. The boudoir of the princess is stated to be exactly as she left it; and it has in truth every appearance of being so. All the exquisite *recherché* of a royal petite maitresse is visible in the whole arrangement. The magnificent chiffoniers, the pretty collection of gems, even the writing-table of the banished lady, remain as she left them. The pens, stained with ink, still hang suspended in their golden cradles; and sundry sheets of paper, edged with black, show that she was still in mourning for her empress mother. Even her gloves, looking as if just drawn off her hands, lie on the table. There is something very melancholy in all this.

To describe each princely chamber, going on *crescendo*, as they do, in splendour, from the first to the last, is quite out of the question. It is useless to say that one room is lined with Italian marble; another hung with crimson velvet, bordered by fringe of gold; and a third, of which the violet-satined walls are sprinkled with stars of silver; or to tell of the golden candlesticks which would make those of Solomon's temple dwindle into littleness. To expatiate upon all this, with the best skill I have, would fail to convey a just idea of this princely dwelling. I may, perhaps, do greater justice to its dazzling magnificence, if I confess, that, for the first time in my life, in a mansion containing good pictures, the decorations and furniture made me forget them. After the first startling effect was past, however, I recovered my senses sufficiently to discover that the collection, though small, is a very fine one.

"C'est fini!" said the guide on reaching the last room, and signifying that we might here leave the list shoes, in which we had made the circuit; "C'est fini!"—and though this was said only with the tone of mock dignity, which these ambulant catalogues often assume, I could not help feeling that, when applied to those tenantless chambers, it sounded like a dirge to the House of Nassau in Belgium.

We visited the little Mint; and were introduced to the master of it by Mr. C. W****, a lively and intelligent Englishman, well known, I believe, in the literary world, and a resident of long standing in Brussels. His obliging attentions to us were particularly acceptable, as he was quite *au-fait* of every thing best worth being seen and heard. This master of the mint seemed born to flourish in a revolutionary era, and to possess the power of turning his faculties, certainly of no mean order, into whatever channel the stormy current of the times might open before him. He had been a minister of state, an officer in the army, and I know not how many things beside: but now he is assiduously occupied in giving his personal superintendence to the making of five-franc pieces and cents. He attended us through the whole establishment; and his manner gave me the idea of a man whose range of talent was far above the common.

The geographical establishment of the MM. Vandermaelen ought to be visited by all foreigners who can procure an introduction to them. For this pleasure we were also indebted to Mr. W. I have never seen a finer example of the pure, enthusiastic love of science, and of a desire to push it into active utility, than in these two brothers. Neither my limits nor my learning suffice to do justice to their establishment by any description I can give of it; and I must therefore content myself by repeating, that all who can obtain permission to visit them will do well to avail themselves of it.

Another introduction, which we owed to the active kindness of the same gentleman, was to M. Robyns. I should imagine that the bump of collectiveness must be very preternaturally developed in this gentleman; and had not his ruling passion been rendered " lawful as eating" by a large fortune and unbounded liberality, I think he must perforce have become a thief, as renowned as Schinderhannes himself; for his mansion and garden render it clearly evident that such an acquisitive rabia must have been satisfied in some way or other. Mr. W. first expressed a wish that we should see his collection of sparrows; and we were led into his garden, (which, for its size, contains also a good collection of exotic plants,) and thence to a sort of open arcade at one side of it. Here a most singular spectacle met our eyes. The walls and ceiling are covered by the carcasses of innumerable little birds, nailed into every imaginable vagary of form—stars, crescents, crosses, all packed close together with such cautious economy of space, that thousands and thousands of little twitterers must have been sacrificed to make up the show.

"By what means, Monsieur," said I, "have you been enabled to collect such an astonishing number of little birds?"

"I rise with the sun every morning of the year, Madame," was the satisfactory reply; "my first care is to set nets the whole length of this gravel walk; I then place myself in that chair, with the string of the net in my hand for a certain number of hours, according to the season. The result is the collection you see."

We then entered the house, where we were soon after joined by so very agreeable a party of English, that I shall long remember the acquaintance made in M. Robyns' museum with pleasure. The business of exhibition proceeded: but were I to rehearse one-hundredth part of the things brought in review before us, I should find faith in none, from the impossibility that any, who have not seen, should believe, how many millions of objects may be crammed into a limited space by the force of a strong collective genius.

"Soyez amant, et vous serez inventif," says La Fontaine. Nothing is more true. A passionate love of bringing things together has inspired M. Robyns with contrivances to lodge his treasures, that almost equal in ingenuity the space-saving arrangement of a honeycomb. Were this gentleman's collection divided into many, each containing objects illustrative of one branch of science or art, the astonishing accumulation would be better appreciated. As it is, nothing is seen well, from the necessity of looking at something else.

"Shall I show you my collection of butterflies, ladies?"

And in a moment a hundred drawers were protruded from the walls, and a hundred cases were opened in the hollows of window-shutters and the interstices of doorways, containing the richest and rarest assemblage of jewelled insects that I ever looked upon.

"Or do you prefer moths?"

And before we had half gratified our eyes with the brilliant spectacle contained in every one of the butterfly repositories, they were withdrawn, and, by some inconceivable contrivance, more drawers and more cases seemed to issue from the same places, containing all the moth family, from gaily-coloured monsters as large as a bat, to milk-white midges that required a magnifying glass. These too were well worth long and patient examination;

but in a moment we were withdrawn from them by a demand, whether we liked engravings?

"Here is the whole Musée Napoleon;" and, "here are all the caricatures published in Paris for the last thirty years." "Here is Piranesi—a particularly fine copy;" and, "here——by the by, ladies, I believe I have the largest collection of music in the world; if you will just step *par ici* I will show it to you."

In this way we obtained in the course of a few hours a very tantalizing conviction, that M. Robyns had a prodigious number of things worth seeing, but that it was quite impossible to find time to look at them.

After a morning of much amusement the whole party accompanied Mr. W. to the restaurant of the justly-celebrated Du Bos, where he gave us as elegant an entertainment as can well be imagined. It was very evident that whatever confusion the revolution had produced in other departments, that of the *cuisine* showed no symptom of unseemly innovation or incongruous combination. Everything was in perfectly good style; and I have seldom been present at a more agreeable entertainment.

The theatre at Brussels is neither very large nor very splendid; nor was the company of performers so good as I had expected to find in a continental capital. It did not appear to be the fashionable resort at the period of our visit; for the house was not elegantly filled either of the two evenings we went there.

Nothing can be more easy and agreeable than the style of the Brussels parties. A few distinguished individuals give dinners, from which the gentlemen and ladies rise together; and after a cup of exquisite *café noir*, taken in the drawing-room, they separate to amuse themselves elsewhere.

Many English families have handsome houses, well calculated for receiving company; and all lying so near together round the park and Boulevard de Namur, as to render the attending the evening *réunions*, constantly given in many of them, perfectly easy even without a carriage. I had the pleasure of being at several of these parties in two or three different houses, and found the style of them very like that of Paris undressed soirées. Sometimes the young people stand up to waltz; but in general, music, cards, and conversation occupy the hours.

I saw a good many gay equestrians, both male and female, and looking very Hyde-parkish, enjoying the beautiful gallop of the Boulevard; and the park also at the fashionable hour for walking was never without some elegant-looking group: nevertheless, all agreed in assuring me that Brussels was no longer what it had been.

The old town has many fine Gothic buildings, particularly the cathedral church of St. Gudule, and the Hôtel de Ville. The great market-place, in which this last is situated, equals, or perhaps surpasses, everything we have seen in Belgium for the picturesque effect of its fine old buildings. If I visit Brussels again, I think that for one week I will have my domicile in the lower town, that the brilliant attractions of the upper may not prevent my seeing thoroughly all the rich old remnants of Brabant splendour, which are to be found in all the ancient parts of the city.

We spent one long day at Louvain, and saw all that one day could show; which, in a place where objects of interest lie so closely together as they do there, was a great deal. We passed an hour in the courts and halls of the University; went into many handsome rooms containing its large library; left not a school or lecture-room unvisited; and yet, excepting the old woman who was our guide through them, we saw not a human being in the University of Louvain.

The whole town appeared to me to look desolate and untenanted. The cathedral church of St. Peter is magnificent; and the pulpit one of the finest specimens extant of the lost art of carving in wood. The form of the structure is somewhat pyramidical, representing at the base the conversion of St. Paul, in which the figures, horse included, are as large as life; and finished at the top by two elegantly-branching palm trees, which bend over the canopy of the pulpit. Several cherubims are floating about this canopy with a degree of life and grace quite astonishing in such a material. This magnificent work formerly ornamented the archiepiscopal church at Mechlin, but was removed to Louvain at the time of the revolution.

The splendid tabernacle, in which the elements of the Eucharist are enshrined in the church, is most superbly carved in white stone. It is of great height, and covered with scriptural groups in very fine alto relievo.

The celebrated Hôtel de Ville of Louvain is so well known by drawings, engravings, and descriptions, that all I need add is an acknowledgment that its fame is well merited. It is by far the richest piece of Gothic work I ever saw.

Our drive back to Brussels was delightfully cool and refreshing after a fatiguing day; and, for the first time since our arrival in the gay little metropolis, we retired early to rest.

Another day was given to an excursion into the country, for the purpose of seeing something of the environs, and particularly the pretty villa of Teroueren, belonging to the Prince of Orange. This is another splendid specimen of the elegant taste of its owner; but there is something too melancholy in walking through these silent and forsaken halls, and in meditating on the feelings of those who have been obliged to leave the chosen palaces " in which they made them glad." The gardens are large and handsome, but not very picturesque; nor is there any great beauty in the surrounding country. The road from Brussels passes through an extensive wood; and the effects of light and shade athwart the long avenues form the best feature of the drive.

It was no easy matter to fix the day of departure from Brussels. We had old friends to leave there, long valued and long lost, who had made it their home; we had to say farewell to many new acquaintance, whose gracious and graceful kindness would have made a longer enjoyment of it very agreeable: but already one month of our summer had slipped away, and, though conscious that the interesting old city had not been half explored, we resolutely decided upon leaving it.

Part of our last morning was devoted to taking as general a view of the town as the time permitted. The most remarkable objects we had before visited, but I had hitherto formed no very accurate idea of the whole. No contrast in style and effect can be more perfect than that between the upper and lower town. The former is airy, gay, brilliant, and entirely modern; the latter close, dark, sombre, and venerable: both have charms for the traveller, though of a kind widely different.

It must be confessed, however, that the cheerful aspect of the new town is, for the present, greatly injured by the traces of revolutionary violence, which are suffered to remain so strangely unobliterated in the very centre of its splendour. The residence of Count Crockenberg, close to the royal palace, is a mass of ruins. The park, as the handsome area is called round which the principal buildings are erected, is in many places fenced with hurdles; while in others the handsome Tuileries-like railings remain. I will also confess that, to my taste, the tree of liberty, as the symbol of anarchy is called, rearing its lank, uncomely height, " like a tall bully," before the windows of the king's palace, is by no means a graceful addition to the scene. Its branches, however, are withering, and looked very much as if the sap had ceased to flow. Perhaps at my next visit I may see a kingly statue erected in its place.

Chapter IV.

Waterloo—St. Jean—Belle Alliance—Monuments—Road to Namur—Namur—Huy—Pensionnat—Citadel—Liège—Quentin Durward—Churches—Chaudfontaine—Belgian Politics.

Notwithstanding the twenty years, or near it, which have passed since Waterloo was the spot of earth to which all Europe looked with the most lively interest, all my English feelings were as much awakened at the idea of seeing it, as if its glory had arisen but yesterday. Though I am aware that the subject is "somewhat musty," and decidedly out of fashion, yet I must venture to give a few words to it. A mile before we reached the ground, we were addressed on each side of the carriage by men who offered to be our guides over it: women, too, with baskets on their arms containing relics of the battle, came crowding round us, offering imperial eagles, bullets, and brass buttons for sale. One might easily have fancied the event to which they all referred had taken place a short month before. We had been cautioned not to stop at the village, though its name made it difficult to obey; but, in fact, the battle-ground is too far from Waterloo to permit its being reached from thence by a walk. We therefore persuaded our coachman, though not very easily, to take us on to Mont St. Jean, a little hamlet of the same parish, nearly a league farther, in which are several detached farms; and in the fields surrounding these was lost and won the most important battle that ever was fought. On arriving at this hamlet, we found, contrary to the assurances of our driver, a very decent little inn, close to all the objects we wished to examine, and immediately accepted the services of a guide, recommended by our host, to lead us among them. We could not have fallen into better hands: he was sixteen years old when the engagement took place; and had been an active agent in the scenes which followed it. He was employed, as he told us, for many hours of the day in carrying water to the wounded; and towards evening had ministered to the wants of the more fortunate; to whom a substantial meal, however rude, was all that was wanting to make them the most contented as well as the most triumphant of mortals.

The weather was intensely hot; and the plain we had to walk over utterly without shade; but this good fellow contrived to beguile the way wonderfully well. I know not whether he had tact enough to teach him that such anecdotes would be particularly agreeable; but he gave us more than one beautiful story of British tenderness, generosity, and fortitude. If, however, our Belgian friend intends to be equally agreeable to all the English travellers who may still pause on their way to look at Waterloo, he must study a page of their politics, which it was evident had not yet been opened to him.

" Votre Duc de Wellington était là," said he, pointing to a spot near us; " je l'ai vu, moi, entouré de ses généraux. Mon Dieu! Quel homme! J'étais tout près de lui ici—justement ici—et lui, il était là. Quel homme! et comme tous ses officiers le regardaient. N'est-ce-pas qu'il est adoré en Angleterre?"

My cheeks tingled as I remembered the windows of Apsley House; and I would not have been obliged to tell that poor fellow, in his rusty, *blouze* what he would see if he came to gaze on the dwelling of the hero of Waterloo, for more than I will say.

"Oui, mon ami, oui," was my reply; and if I spoke not truth, the sin will rest on other heads than mine.

In the course of our progress, we were led to the monument raised to the Hanoverians who fell; and to that erected to the memory of Sir Alexander Gordon. But the most striking object on the field of Waterloo is the stupendous mound piled by the King of Holland over the spot where his son the Prince of Orange was wounded. It is a pyramid of 250 feet high, and employed 200 men constantly for three years.

Considering the sad numbers who breathed their souls out on the same battle-ground, to whom not even a grassy hillock rises, marking the spot where they fell, this colossal memorial of the royal soldier's wound seemed somewhat too predominant. It struck me, moreover, that if living bravery be thus permitted to witness its own renown, it would not be amiss to ask permission of King Leopold for the erection of a statue to the Duke of Wellington. As the thought occurred, I fixed upon the spot where I would have it rise; it was the bit of elevated ground on which he stood when his genius directed the bold and decisive movements which made the conqueror of the world stand aghast. A massive bronze statue on this spot would show well against the sky; and, as my fancy conjured it up before me, methought it was classically draped, after the manner of John Kemble, with an attitude and air which recalled the idea of Coriolanus.

We mounted to the top of the pyramid by steps so rudely cut as to render the enterprise one of some difficulty; but were rewarded by overlooking the field of battle in a manner to give a much more comprehensive idea of its arrangement than could be obtained below. Our guide was a very intelligent chronicler, and pointed out with great animation the points where the tug of war had been the strongest.

The bronze lion on its summit, which was fabricated at Liege, is a magnificent monster, measuring twenty feet from head to tail, and looked, as our guide remarked, proudly enough towards France.

After descending from this artificial mountain, which was very nearly as difficult as climbing up it, we traversed the plain in all directions; and, spite of the burning mid-day sun, left no spot unvisited to which any record of peculiar interest was attached.

Not all that has been said and written on the subject—not all the years that have passed since that great day arose—could lessen the interest we felt at finding ourselves standing on the ground whose fame had been so long familiar to us.

Who could be told, without feeling some swelling at the heart, "There, where you now stand, stood your Wellington—here were his officers all round him—yonder was the farthest point to which Napoleon advanced—and it was there he uttered his last command, '*Sauve qui peut!*'"

The ruin of the Château of Hougoumont is, I think, the most interesting point of all. The struggle was there perhaps the fiercest; the battered walls, the dismantled and fire-stained chapel, which remained standing through all the wreck, and where they show a crucifix, that, as they say, repeatedly caught fire, but never was consumed,— the traces of attack upon attack, still renewed and still resisted—all, together, bring the whole scene before one with a tremendous force. In the garden of Hougoumont is one solitary tomb raised over the body of Captain Blackman. He was buried exactly where he fell—

"With his martial cloak around him,"

and his monument is the only one so erected.

At length, sufficiently heated and weary to make the sight of the little inn extremely welcome, we reached *La Belle Alliance*, over the door of which it is recorded that within its humble walls Wellington and Blucher met, and reposed, on the evening of the ever-memorable 18th June, 1815.

As I sat down in the little whitewashed parlour

where the first triumphant, yet melancholy hour that succeeded the battle was passed by the victorious Generals, I fancied I saw them surrounded by their staff, waiting with trembling eagerness to learn who among their brave companions still lived to share their triumph. It was in this room that they heard the names of all the brave spirits who had paid their lives for the mighty prize their country had won; and it was here that the first and most precious tribute of gratitude and of sorrow embalmed the memory of the slain.

We returned to our little inn about three o'clock; and gladly welcomed the shade of its humble parlour. Our walk had altogether been so long and fatiguing, and the heat continued to be so overpowering, that I reposed for some hours before I ventured out again: but towards evening large masses of heavy summer clouds rolled together; and though the air was stifling, there was at least no longer sunshine to dread: once more, therefore, I walked out upon the field; my companions had wandered farther, and I was quite alone. Having passed the morning in listening to the brave but bloody deeds it had witnessed, I almost trembled to find myself alone there. The spot was an awful one, and no great stretch of imagination seemed necessary to people it; moreover, the heavy gloom of an approaching storm hung upon every object, and a poet might easily have fancied that the air was darkened by the waving banners of a spectre host careering over it. The day ended by the only violent thunderstorm we encountered during the whole summer.

The next morning, being fortunate enough to find vacant places in a public carriage going from Namur to Brussels, we availed ourselves of it to return to the village of Waterloo. It was Sunday, and we heard mass performed in the little church, whose walls are lined with the memorials erected in honour of the brave men who perished near it. After mass we walked with a guide about the village, and visited many spots made memorable by having some connexion or other with the battle.

The object, whose display was preluded with the most ceremony, was a sort of mausoleum, bearing the following inscription :—

> "Ci est enterrée la jambe
> De l'illustre et vaillant Comte Uxbridge,
> Lieutenant-Général de S. M. Britannique,
> Commandant en chef la cavalerie
> Anglaise, Belge, et Hollandaise,
> Blessé le 18 Juin, 1815,
> A la mémorable bataille de Waterloo,
> Qui, par son héroïsme, a concouru au triomphe
> De la cause du genre humain,
> Glorieusement décidée par l'éclatante
> Victoire
> Du dit jour."

On each side of this inscription was a tablet bearing another: that to the right ran thus—

> "Cet endroit fut visité le 1er Octobre, 1821,
> Par George IV. roi de la Grande Bretagne;"

that on the left,

> "Cet endroit fut visité le 20 Septembre, 1825,
> Par S. M. le roi de Prusse, accompagné de
> Trois princes, ses fils."

No one, I think, can help feeling that this singular shrine is not that on which the names of the royal pilgrims could with the most propriety have been engraved: yet it is the only one at Waterloo which bears records of their visits. There is something disagreeably approaching to the bathos, in passing from the graves of buried heroes to the repository of a severed limb. Had this brave and noble soldier left no other memorial of his presence at Waterloo than his leg, this strange devotion to it would be less annoying. Whoever they were who testified the fervour of their admiration by raising this singular mausoleum, they would have done better, had they trusted, for the recollection of the event, to the fame of the noble and well-remembered firmness with which Lord Anglesey bore his loss: but as the leg itself was most assuredly the member to which the brave nobleman was the least likely to be indebted on the field of battle, some portion of the circumstance and ceremony respecting it might have been well spared.

We dined at l'Hôtel du Roi d'Angleterre, and then took the coupé, which we had previously engaged, in the diligence for Namur. We passed by Quatre-bras, where Blucher was defeated on the 17th—the day before the decisive battle; and also by the well-known village of Genappe. About two leagues before reaching Namur, our eyes were refreshed by the first picturesque landscape we had looked upon since we entered Belgium.

A little bright, meandering stream, a beetling

rock of mountain limestone hanging over it, with a most Udolpho-like-looking castle in the woods beyond, formed a perfect treat for three picturesque-seeking travellers, who, for the last month, had seen nothing but the level plains of Flanders, Antwerp, and Brabant.

All the large farm-houses in this neighbourhood have been evidently constructed with a view to defence. They almost always enclose a square: the outsides of the barns, which form the walls of it, are very substantially built of stone, having loop-holes at regular distances round the whole extent: the gates are high, and frequently embattled, with a huge portal, calculated to resist every thing except artillery.

The approach to Namur is magnificent. The town lies in a basin at the juncture of the Sambre and the Meuse. At the angle formed by this "meeting of the waters" is the bold, abrupt termination of the long range of hills running between them; and on the summit of this lofty eminence stands the citadel with its superb works, stretching over the whole face of the mountain.

The cathedral church of St. Aubaine, and also

St. Loup, are well seen in approaching the city: but the hills which rise so nobly in all directions round it, prevent any building but the dominating citadel from producing great effect. A nearer examination does not, however greatly increase the idea of their architectural beauty: neither is the town well built; nor are the streets either very clean or very fragrant. We had recently seen too many splendid churches for those of Namur to inspire much admiration: that of St. Loup is the best worth seeing, for the sake of its very singular and beautifully carved roof of stone.

Namur had, however, attractions for my son, which, unhappily, my ignorance prevented my sharing. In his opinion, the collection of M. Cauchy, to whom M. Vandermaelen had given him a letter, is one of the most perfect, in the objects it has been his purpose to collect, that can any where be seen. It contains a complete collection of specimens illustrative of the geology of Belgium. I heard most honourable mention of the *savoir* of a fair countrywoman; several fossil shells in the collection having *been determined*,

M. Cauchy said, by Mrs. M——n. As I have the pleasure of knowing, from my own observation, that this accomplished lady "wears her faculties so meekly," as in no degree to let them interfere with her kindness to the less informed of her own sex, I listened with the more pleasure to the admiration expressed for her unusual scientific information; and heartily lamented that, in my own case, "knowledge by this entrance" was so completely shut out.

After passing a day at Namur, we embarked on board a little dirty packet-boat, which navigates the Meuse from thence to Huy. We had been particularly desired not to omit this pretty voyage; and in truth we found that it deserved all the praise bestowed on it: but it is only the more to be regretted that the total want of every thing like decent accommodation on board the boats should be such as completely to turn pleasure into pain.

Whoever travels this route, with a leisure day or two to spare, will do well to spend them at Huy. The Meuse is here at its handsomest width, and has a little rapid below the bridge, occasioning a lively movement of its waters, which here at least deserve not the epithet of " sluggish." The hills, which rise on either side, are bold and picturesque; and on one of these the citadel of Huy rears its massive front, sometimes crowning the rock, and sometimes permitting naked crags to rise amidst the masonry, and become a part of its strength. Below the citadel, and stretching its noble length eastward, stands the cathedral; somewhat injured by repeated innovations, but lofty, venerable, and imposing: below this is the beautiful grey stone bridge, with its seven graceful arches: and turn the eye in what direction you will, some tower, some convent, or some old grotesque Burgundian mansion greets you, all in those mellowed tints of red and grey, so dear to Prout. One cause of this peculiarly picturesque aspect is, that the little town of Huy, containing only five thousand inhabitants, boasts sixteen churches and monasteries. The guide-books say, that no town in the world of the same dimensions has so many edifices of the kind, or so many priests residing in it. I inquired of an inhabitant, with whom we made acquaintance, if this were so. "Ma foi, oui," was the reply; "il n'y a pas à redire à cela, et le bon Dieu en prends soin; car, si tout le monde manque de quoi vivre, les prêtres ne manquent de rien."

The walks on both sides of the Maese were so beautiful, and we heard such interesting stories of monasteries, still containing venerable remnants of their once numerous sisterhoods, that we decided upon passing another day, for the purpose of exploring the country, and, if possible, of entering one of these holy sanctuaries.

Having mounted a hill on the western side of the river, we perceived a building, which, from its Gothic chapel, lofty walls, and air of deep seclusion, we felt assured must be a nunnery. We eagerly approached it; and, on ringing the great bell at the outer gate, a female in black answered it. She did not look exactly like a nun, but still she might be a lay sister. Her linen was religiously white, and her hair invisible: so, nothing doubting, we requested permission, as strangers, to see the house. The supposed nun answered very civilly, "Entrez, s'il vous plait; je vais voir." We advanced, and found ourselves in a venerable cloister, the centre of which was converted into a pretty flower-garden. Here we remained for a few minutes, congratulating each other upon having found our way into such sacred precincts. Presently the same female returned, and invited us to follow her, which we did, through several long passages, vaulted and echoing to our hearts' desire: at length we were ushered into a parlour; but, alas! it was without a *grille*; and we were received by a lady, whom all our predetermination to find ourselves in a convent could not enable us to mistake for a nun. She welcomed us, however, with the greatest civility; declared she should have much pleasure in showing us the establishment; and displayed some beautiful embroidery and several drawings, far from contemptible. I felt rather ashamed of our intrusion; and having given a just tribute of praise to the elegant labours of her scholars, attempted to bow a retreat: but she so earnestly requested me to permit her to show us the house, that it was impossible to refuse; and accordingly we all followed her through the various parts of the building; which had, in truth, a few years before, been a large and handsome convent. On her opening the door of a long dormitory, filled with double rows of little white beds, I stopped but a moment to admire their neatness, and retreated to the gallery, very truly ashamed of giving her so much unnecessary trouble; but she took me by the arm, and led me again into the room, saying, " Permettez moi, Madame; Messieurs, entrez s'il vous plait—il faut voir tout;" and I almost suspected that, notwithstanding her great civility, she meant to make us perform a little penance for our impertinent curiosity. But I did her great injustice, for she led us on through the long chamber with a far different purpose, and opening a pair of folding-doors at the end of it, said, in a voice that seemed to challenge both admiration and reverence, " Voilà notre église!" She crossed herself as she spoke, and then stood aside, as if to watch the effect of the scene upon us.

The *coup-d'œil* was really very striking. The large gallery in which we stood looked into a handsome chapel of great antiquity: the altar, which faced us, was showily decorated and embellished, as well as many little shrines along the walls, with a profusion of newly-gathered flowers. The whole floor seemed paved with the grave-stones of the deceased sisters, varied at intervals by one of superior ornament and dignity, indicating the resting-place of an abbess. I thought, as I looked at these memorials, that if any of the little ladies, who slept in the room which opened upon them, were subject to superstitious fears, they might sometimes feel uncomfortable from the gloomy proximity: but, excepting this visionary objection, the Pensionnat, into which we had so unceremoniously intruded ourselves, seemed a very desirable place of education; possessing, over and above all others, the very remarkable advantage of including all charges in the sum of four hundred francs; and as the "*carte de renseignements*" expressed it, "*pas d'autre dépense sous quelque dénomination que ce puisse être.*"

After this pilgrimage we returned to the town, and obtained permission to visit the citadel. This is still a virgin fortress, and was built by the King of Holland, under the direction, as we were told, of an English engineer. All the public works of this monarch seem boldly conceived and magnificently executed. A thousand workmen were employed for eight years in completing the citadel of Huy. I have had but few opportunities of comparing such kind of buildings with each other, but this is by far the most stupendous piece of masonry I ever saw. The living rock, indeed, has been made to obey the bold design of the engineer; and it is by excavation, almost as much as by building, that this fortress has obtained its reputation of almost unequalled strength.

Over one of the massive gateways is the following motto:—

> Etiamsi fractus illabatur orbis
> Impavidum ferient ruinæ.

The country between Huy and Liege, though beautiful to eyes that had not yet forgotten the plains of Flanders, was much less so than between Huy and Namur. I know no city the entrance to which is less inviting than that of Liege; every object seems more or less stained by the hue of coal. My son, indeed, looked from the windows of the carriage, and exclaimed, in a tone of singular satisfaction, " Here we are again on the coal measures!" but to me, this only seemed to confirm the idea that we were in danger of suffocation from coal dust.

We passed some handsome houses, with gardens well laid out; but the walks were neatly-rolled small coal. Our postilion cracked his whip, as we entered the city, and the accelerated crunching of coals beneath our wheels responded to it; and, in short, not all my anticipations of pleasure from becoming acquainted with a place so famed in story could prevent me, as I drove into the town, from earnestly longing to drive out of it again.

The next morning, however, my imagination being, I suppose, refreshed with sleep, I forgot all present annoyances, while tracing the memorials of the olden times. How much of this might be attributable to the interest we all own in the generations which have played their part and passed away, and how much to feelings connected with a particular individual, named Quentin Durward, I will not pretend to define: but it is certain that there was hardly any part of the city into which visions connected with him did not follow me; and I not only made out to my entire satisfaction the very spot where Gertrude Pavillon led the Scottish Archer through her father's garden to the boat that waited for him on the Maese, but I am quite sure, too, that I know exactly the point at which Quentin left the town to return to the castle of Schonwaldt; and that I should not be far out did I undertake to designate the exact place where he proved himself rather an angel than a man, by leaving the half-won conquest of the boar to rescue the friendly Trudchen.

By the way I was rather amused, while turning over the pages of a modern history of Liege in a bookseller's shop, to find the following passage:—
" C'est ici le lieu de faire un tableau de l'état de la France au quinzième siècle, et de tracer le caractère de Louis XI. J'emprunterai à Sir Walter Scott presque tous les détails que j'ai à donner là-dessus."

The process of converting history into romance is a delightful operation, by which we have all profited; but the value of that by which romance is recreated into history is still to be learned.

The cathedral church, now called St. Paul's,

but originally dedicated to St. Lambert, has some very fine painted glass, and the ceiling is curious from the unusual style of its coloured decorations.

This recalled the manner in which the ceiling of the transepts of Winchester Cathedral has been repaired, and which I remember to have heard censured as incongruous in style; but its exact conformity with this fine old church is a satisfactory proof of their propriety, and of the *savoir* o the learned antiquary who adopted it.

The church of St. Martin stands very finely on the side of a hill that leads towards the citadel. The interior of this church is extremely gaudy as to its ornaments; and adorned besides with a profusion of orange trees, oleanders, and myrtles. One part of its decoration consisted in a large display of framed placards (some of them ornamented with painted wreaths of flowers and other pretty devices), recording a multitude of recent miracles, each of them headed, in large letters, "*Miracle approuvé.*" On one was inscribed "Marie Cornelis, ayant l'œil piqué et traversé d'une épine, en recouvre la vue."

We entered this church while five priests were

engaged in performing mass before a moveable figure of the Virgin, more profusely tricked out in tawdry finery than any figure I have seen.

From thence we climbed Mount Walburgis, and approached, as nearly as we were permitted, to the citadel on the top of it. The paved street, which leads up the side of this height to the fortress, is the steepest elevation I ever saw so used; but the view from the summit well repays the labour of ascending.

The Palais de Justice, formerly the Palais Episcopal, is large and handsome. The Maison de Ville, in the market-place, and the three fountains near it, also deserve to be looked at; but the dismally dirty, dusty atmosphere made it really a task either to drive or walk about the city; and it was with all the enjoyment that the hope of breathing freely could give, that we mounted a *char-à-banc* for the purpose of passing a few hours at Chaudfontaine.

I suspect that this most singularly lovely spot is less known to English travellers than it ought to be; for I have rarely heard it mentioned, except by foreigners: but the little valley, in which the baths that have given the place its name are situated, is alone infinitely better worth taking a journey to see than many objects which yearly draw crowds of tourists from our shores. The baths, of which there are enough to show that they are greatly frequented by the neighbourhood, are in the hands of government; and every thing about them is in the highest degree comfortable, or, rather, luxurious. I certainly never enjoyed a bath so much. The exquisite clearness of the water, the noble size of the marble chamber into which you descend to enjoy it, and its delightful natural temperature (twenty-six degrees of Reaumur), all contribute to make Chaudfontaine the very perfection of a bathing-place. I will not attempt any description of the wooded hills which rise on either side of this fairy valley, nor of the bright stream that ripples through it: I will only say—pass it not by unseen. The distance from Liege is not above seven miles.

The return to our hotel after such an excursion was really terrible, and most gladly did we bid adieu on the following morning to the coal-stained city.

Aix-la-Chapelle was to be our next resting-place, and the Prussian frontier was to be passed about half way to it.

Before leaving Belgium, I must say a few farewell words respecting it. Not many among us are, I believe, fully aware how peculiarly rich this country is in objects of every kind that can most interest and delight a traveller; provided, indeed, that he be not journeying post to the Rhine, but have time and inclination to pause and look about him. People who love pictures know that Flanders possesses many *chef-d'œuvres* of the art; and people who love churches are aware that the Low Countries are famed for Gothic architecture: nevertheless, but few of our yearly tourists pause long enough to enjoy fully the exceeding richness of Belgium in all that can gratify the eye of taste, or " awaken the enthusiasm of the antiquary." Where can be found such a constellation of fine old cities as Bruges, Ghent, Antwerp, Louvain, Brussels, Namur, and Liege? each assisting to illustrate the history of the others, and all within so small a space, that they may be visited in succession, and revisited again half-a-dozen times in the course of as many weeks; and that, perhaps, at a less expense, than if the same time were spent at a fashionable watering-place in England.

Of genuine Flemish manners it is not easy to form any accurate judgment by merely passing a few weeks in the country, and going only into the society that good travelling introductions lead to: for therein will be found the same uniform tone of European good breeding which distinguishes the well-educated from those who are not so, in every country; but which has too little characteristic variety to be considered as purely national in any. I took some pains, and not quite without success, to look a little more behind the scenes, and whenever I did so, the conformity in habits and character of the present race, with the portraits made familiar to us in the history of ages past, was most striking.

It should seem that even the soil and air had an influence on the tailors, stocking-weavers, and shoemakers; for there are still the self-same outlines, nay, the self-same colours, and, as it should seem, the identical materials, with which they wrought. Nor are the healthy, comely, lusty weavers more changed. No people, I think, bear a stronger national impress on their features than the peasants of Flanders; and their admirable painters have made us all sufficiently familiar with them.

Of their manners I saw enough to show me that they were industrious, clean, cheerful, and kind-hearted; and if beer and tobacco-smoke constitute a larger portion of their happiness than might be wished, it should be remembered that it is better to smoke than chew the loathsome herb; and that barley may be taken in a more pernicious form than that of Flemish ale.

Of the ranks immediately above these it is less easy to judge: but perhaps if I abstain from naming the city, where it was made, I may venture to insert the translation of a provincial sketch given me by a lively young French woman, who had resided some years there. Of its accuracy I am hardly competent to give an opinion, though there are some features which *saute aux yeux*, of which I confess the resemblance is striking.

Journal of a Belgian Lady,

(NOT OF THE CAPITAL.)

She rises generally about seven o'clock, provided the children, who all sleep in her room, have permitted her to repose till so late an hour. Her toilet does not take long; a black petticoat being the only addition she makes to the cap and brown cotton wrapping-gown in which she sleeps. In this *equipage,* with one child in her arms, and half-a-dozen following her, she goes down to breakfast; which repast is often taken in the kitchen and lasts but a few moments, amidst cries and quarrellings for slices of bread and butter, and mugs of coffee.

This trouble over, the lady commences the toilet of her little family; an operation which she always performs carefully and neatly, and the children are despatched to school.

A general review of the mansion follows; and woe to the servants if any candle-ends of the preceding night have been burned too low—if a single grain of dust be visible on the furniture, or a cup broken; for crimes of this cast ever become the subject of most vehement reproach.

At length the bell rings for mass; a morning dress, not peculiar for its elegance, succeeds to the first costume; a black cloak and hood is thrown over it; and, with a basket on her arm, she repairs to the church, and from thence to make bargains, and execute commissions.

This period, the happiest of her day, is prolonged till dinner. In the course of her peregrination she meets her acquaintance, and the most innocent little gossipings take place. It is now that she learns how much Mrs. Such-a-one gave beyond what she ought for a turbot; and, consequently, how very bad a manager she must be: while on the other hand, Mrs. Somebody is so stingy, that she stands half an hour higgling about green peas;—Mrs. A. has given her maid warning; Mrs. B. has a sick baby; and the Curé has made a visit at least half an hour long to Miss C.

And now the clock strikes twelve, and dinner leads everybody home. The children have returned from school; the tumult and the din begin again;

and the young ones contrive to render the dinner as miserable as the breakfast. This dinner, however, is eaten in a handsome room, ornamented with mirrors, carpets, and so forth, but none of the thousand and one little prettinesses which constitute elegance and comfort. Everything is handsome and correct; and everything is heavy and gloomy. Its tenants know the wants of animal life, but little more : the dinner is good and abundant, but the conversation—nought.

The meal ended, and the dessert distributed among the children, peace is once more restored by their dismissal to school.

The lady then places herself at her window with her work, which she continues without interruption till she goes to vespers; after which she gives her children their supper and puts them to bed; then undresses herself, puts her hair into papillotes, says her prayers, and, while waiting the return of her spouse, amuses herself by chatting a little with her servants in the kitchen. A well-behaved husband is never later than nine : as soon as he appears, a substantial supper is served, and at ten the whole house is in a state of profound repose.

This life, with very few exceptions, is that of all the ladies of ——————.

If their minds do not greatly improve by it, their plumpness and fresh complexions prove at least that it agrees well with their constitutions. What can they wish for more? Of what use would mind be to them? A Fleming marries in order to have a housekeeper who will not cheat him—his dinner punctually served—his children kept clean—and his stockings mended. He asks for nothing more, and is perfectly contented with this. They are happy. What more can be desired?—nothing; —excepting, perhaps, the not being obliged to witness a happiness so insupportable.

. . . . . .

The scenery of the Sambre and the Meuse is as beautiful as the most devoted lover of landscape can desire: there are points near Liege that may challenge comparison with any scenery of the same class in the world; and I think that I have not yet seen the valley which could be preferred to that of Chaudfontaine.

In addition to all this, the glorious fertility of the agricultural districts well deserves to be mentioned. Were there nothing else to reward a traveller for going thither, I think the sight of the rich fields of Flanders would be enough to do it. It is surely a fair object of curiosity to see what may be the largest quantity of grain that can stand in any given space; and this, I think, may be satisfactorily decided in Belgium.

England has noble fields of grain, and her herbage is rich and abundant; but in Flanders the soil is crammed with produce, and the corn stands on the ground like a solid mass.

In short, Belgium is a beautiful little kingdom; and, notwithstanding the extent of territory be small, it has sufficient within its circuit to give its name a higher rank among the nations of the Continent than its extent of domain alone could justify.

Were the spirit of her present legislators as congenial to the natural temper of her citizens, as the air and soil to the various treasures of her fields, it might be fairly hoped that peace, as well as plenty, would long smile upon them: but there appears to be a restless craving for still further changes among some who have much influence, which promises anything rather than permanent tranquillity.

There are stirring spirits in Belgium, who would willingly work political innovation, not only by the modern process of overturning all constituted authority, but by reviving power, which has long lain dormant there, and which, in most other countries, may be considered as extinguished for ever. There are more Flemish cities than one in which the destruction, or rather the dispersion, of the Jesuits, is openly deplored; and, if I am rightly informed, many efforts are making to organize new orders among the priesthood, that may increase their power and influence. I heard it repeatedly asserted in society, that had King William been a Catholic, or a *less bigoted Protestant*, (such is the language used,) Belgium and Holland could never have been severed. But even those who profess the most perfect satisfaction at the result of the revolution, do not, in general, speak of the present order of things in a tone that promises its long continuance. "Ça ira pour le moment" was a phrase I heard repeated with slight variations in many circles. Nevertheless, were King Leopold to become a Catholic, and France rest contented without any fresh "immortal three days," the "*moment*" may probably be greatly lengthened.

Chapter V.

*Aix-la-Chapelle — Charlemagne — Napoleon — Relics —
King of Prussia — German Politics.*

Perhaps it requires rather a particular attachment to the memory of Charlemagne to feel all the satisfaction that I did in going over the city of Aix-la-Chapelle, and seeking out, with a guide-book in my hand, every trace, whether real or fanciful, that this Prince of Paladins has left there.

No one can deny that there are enough of both to satisfy the most devoted lover of romance; and if the head be but sufficiently crammed with legends of knights and saints, one may almost have the luxury of fancying for a few hours that one is living in the midst of them. I never felt myself in such palpable contact with the ages that are gone, as while thus engaged; and though I am afraid that nothing can be less like the profound investigations of the cautious antiquary, than the poetical reminiscences indulged in during this time, I much doubt if, in the way of enjoyment, any degree of sober learning would answer so well as that sort of feminine *savoir* obtained through the medium of romance, and which enabled me to see not only all that was to be seen, but, spite of the dictum in the Critic, a great deal more. Without this delightful sort of second-sight, I might have doubted the truth of many interesting particulars, the belief in which exceedingly enhanced my gratification; and I therefore recommend an assiduous perusal both of Berni and Ariosto, to all travellers about to visit this venerable city.

There must be, however, something sufficiently stirring, even to the sober feelings of the antiquary and historian, while standing under the dome of the magnificent cathedral at Aix-la-Chapelle, and hearing, "This is the chapel built by Charlemagne, and under that stone he was buried."

I wished to believe that he lay there still, but this was impossible; for the singular history of his disinterment is one of the most prominent legends of the spot. He had been buried three hundred years, when the Emperor Frederick Barbarossa took him from the tomb. This strange sacrilege is spoken of in the history of Aix as "*une fête touchante*" given by Frederick to the town in 1165 when the embalmed hero was raised from the grave by the Archbishop of Cologne and the Bishop of Liege, and exposed "*à la vénération publique.*"

He was found buried in royal robes, and seated in a chair of marble, with the Gospels on his knees, his sword beside him, and a small casket, containing a portion of the earth which received the blood of the martyred St. Stephen, at his feet. After this "*touchante fête,*" the body of Charlemagne was deposited in a very elegant antique sarcophagus of alabaster, on which the Rape of Proserpine is chiselled in fine relief.

This beautiful coffin is still shown, but no vestige of the illustrious dead remains within it. It is supposed that bone after bone has been taken away, being considered as holy relics; and it is stated that one solitary fragment, saved from this traffic, has been re-interred in the vault from whence his body was removed.

The vast stone that seals this vault, and which

is placed immediately under the centre of the dome, has the words CAROLO MAGNO inscribed upon it. The sacristan, who went over the church with us, told me that he had accompanied Napoleon and Josephine into every part of the building: they were followed, he said, by a numerous cortège of the staff. When Napoleon read these words, he retreated from the verge of the stone, rendered sacred by such an inscription, and having remained for a moment to gaze upon it, walked slowly round, without placing his foot within its limits, but with his eyes still fixed on the venerated name.

"Il y avait quelque-chose de bien frappant dans son regard," said the man, "mais aussi quelque-chose de bien drôle dans l'insouciance avec laquelle ses officiers suivaient ses pas, en évitant de toucher la pierre; mais pourtant, sans avoir l'air de partager du tout son sentiment."

The marble chair in which the body of Charlemagne was found, as well as the royal symbols that were buried with him, have been since used at the coronation of eleven emperors.

A vast gallery runs round the octagon of Charlemagne's chapel, from whence branch off sundry large oriels, forming what is called the Hoch Munster, or upper church. In that division of the octagon gallery, which fronts the high altar below, is placed this sepulchral chair; and it is here that the emperors have been seated to receive the *sacre*, while the electors stood round the gallery, between porphyry pillars, which supported its roof. Some handsome columns still mark the places where these porphyry pillars stood, but the originals went the way of all art, by the order of Napoleon; and though many treasures of the church (not holy relics), which shared the same fate, were returned after the battle of Waterloo, these rich and rare pillars still remain at the Louvre.

When our guide removed the oaken case which covers it, I sat down in the dead man's chair, upon which he told me that Josephine also had placed herself, "while the Emperor stood *there* with his arms crossed upon his breast, looking at her."

It was in a tone which seemed modestly to confess its want of high antiquity, that we were informed the choir of the church was not more than seven hundred years old; but I forgave its recent date in favour of its beauty: it is simple, lofty, light, and elegant.

A little golden crown and sceptre, for the figure of the Virgin at the altar, and still smaller ones for the infant on her arm, are pointed out as an offering from Mary Queen of Scots.

Over the stone inscribed with the name of Charlemagne is suspended an enormous crown of silver gilt, the gift of Frederick Barbarossa: it forms a lustre of forty-eight lights, and is a beautiful and highly-curious specimen of the goldsmith's art of the twelfth century.

People from all quarters of the world have for ages considered themselves as more holy if at any period of their lives they have made the *Achfahrt*, or pilgrimage, to the münster of Charlemagne at Aix; and the wealth which their offerings have brought to the church is immense. No shrine in the world, I believe, boasts so many relics of first-rate sanctity as this. These sacred treasures are divided into two classes, distinguished as the great and the little relics. The first class are exhibited every seventh year, from the 10th to the 24th of July; and some centuries ago, the pilgrims, who came to visit there, were so numerous that the town could not contain the hundredth part of them, and the fields for miles round were converted into stations of rest and refreshment. It is recorded that in the year 1496 no less than 142,000 persons arrived in one day to make their offerings. We had not the good fortune to arrive on the seventh year, and therefore only know by hearsay evidence that they consist of a chemise of the Virgin Mary, the swaddling clothes of the infant Jesus, the linen cloth which received the head of John the Baptist, the scarf worn by the Saviour at the crucifixion, and a small portion of the manna of the desert. These were all sent to Charlemagne by the Patriarch of Jerusalem in the year 799. I was told by a citizen who had often had the advantage of beholding it, that the chemise of the Virgin was of most prodigious size, quite long enough for a person seven feet high. As for the little relics, they are displayed to all comers, and consist of a vast variety of treasures, both sacred and profane.

The article which interested me the most amongst these was the ivory hunting-horn of Charlemagne : it is ornamented with gold, on which are repeatedly engraved the words " Mein ! Ein ! "

The Hôtel de Ville stands on a part of the ground once occupied by the palace in which Charlemagne was born; and one of the towers, called the tower of Granus, is said not only to have been a part of his dwelling, but to have stood there long before, being decidedly of Roman construction. A bronze statue of this mighty king stands in the market-place before the Hôtel de Ville: it is a work of the fourteenth century.

It is not difficult, I believe, for a notable, persevering, check-defying antiquary to trace the course of the external walls of the old palace. They extend far and wide, and pass through the inclosures of many private dwellings. It appears that Charlemagne was particularly attached to this city, and declared it the second in his empire. The inscription upon his palace was—

> Hic sedes regni trans Alpes habeatur caput
> Omnium provinciarum et civitatum Galliæ.

Independent of all these memorials of history and romance, Aix-la-Chapelle is a beautiful and interesting town. Its hot springs are abundant, and held to be highly salubrious. The one which is of the highest temperature rises at Borcette, a little town perfectly distinct from Aix, but close to it. This Borcette spring is much too hot for the hand to endure; but I doubt its being actually boiling, as I have heard stated. We saw, however, several women take pails of it for their washing, and were told that they never find it necessary to use any other in the process. The large smoking caldron, which is open in the middle of the street at Borcette, has a very strange appearance, the vapour rising, and spreading up and down it, to a considerable distance.

A gentleman, to whom we brought a letter of introduction, kindly accompanied us in a beautiful drive round the town. The Louisberg is a singular hill, rising very abruptly from the plain, and commanding a magnificent view. The forest of Ardennes makes an interesting feature in this fine landscape. On and about this pretty little mountain are various memorials of Napoleon and his family. Josephine and Pauline have given their names to temples, groves, and gates. The public walks begun by Napoleon, and completed by the present King of Prussia, are beautiful in no common degree.

It was here that I first heard the name of the King of Prussia pronounced with that emphatic love, reverence, and admiration, which met us so frequently afterwards in the course of our travels through his dominions. I do not speak of the strong personal attachment of his nobles; but whoever will take the trouble of conversing with the lower and middling classes in Prussia will hear their wise and good monarch spoken of as the father of his people.

Had I travelled through the country half a century ago, it is probable that even an equal expression of attachment to the sovereign would not have struck me so forcibly. Loyalty was not then so rare and precious a plant as it has since become; and to feel a glow of universal satisfaction at the heart, because a good king was spoken of with love and reverence by his people, would have been hardly less extravagant, than if one had fallen into a rapture at hearing a son speak with affection of his father.

> "For it so falls out
> That what we have we prize not to the worth,
> Whiles we enjoy it; but being lacked and lost,
> Why then we reck the value."

While remarking on the strong feeling of attachment expressed by all classes to the King of Prussia, I am naturally led to mention the general result of my endeavours to discover the real state of political feeling in the countries through which we travelled. To facilitate this object, I repeatedly accepted introductions from persons whose speculations had, I well knew, led them very far from what I considered to be the principles of political wisdom. I did so from the wish of hearing those subjects fairly discussed abroad which are so constantly thrust into all companies at home; and in the expectation of obtaining, in the intercourse of general society, a more just idea of popular feeling than we can hope to obtain from all our newspapers, whether domestic or foreign: but notwithstanding I thus threw myself in the way of what are called *liberal principles*, I never, except in one solitary instance, heard any sentiments or opinions expressed, in the slightest degree approaching to the mad licentiousness of doctrine which is weekly and daily poured forth by the presses of England.

We are continually told by these that there is a spirit abroad in Germany, which, in the fulness of time, is to bring forth revolution; that massacre and rapine shall engender liberty and peace; and that, in a few short years, all the nations of the earth are to be levelled into one vast ocean of equality.

Should this prophecy be fulfilled, the completion of it will not owe its origin to Germany. Not one of the various dynasties, whether great or small, included in that term, hold rule over a population disposed to seek their happiness or their glory in universal equality. There is a high-spirited and very noble sort of ambition about them, more likely to show itself in efforts to raise their native thrones and sceptres above all others on the earth than to trample the least atom of their dignity in the dust. Instead, therefore, of listening with blind faith to statements as false as they are absurd, it would better become the wisdom of Englishmen to look out, with a feeling of emulation, at least, if not of fear, at the enormous strides which that magnificent country is making to outstrip us in arts and commerce, in learning and in wealth. While we are mouthing out bombastic declamations upon liberty, they are quietly studying the profoundest theories of state policy; and while we avowedly endeavour to make the ark of our government (the only security by which we hold our lives and property) drive along by the current of popular tumult, their rulers sit on high, marking the signs of the times, and making use of the light that is spread abroad, to steer their noble vessel on its course.

One remarkable feature of difference between my own dear country, as seen in these latter days, and the land through which I was travelling, struck me very painfully. At home, I had of late been accustomed to hear every voice from the class emphatically styled *the people*, whether heard through the medium of the press, or in listening to their conversation, expressive of contempt and dislike for their own country, its institutions, and laws. The same class that I remember, in early youth, to have heard splitting the skies in *vivats* to their own glory, now mutter curses on the church of their fathers, and almost deprecate the flag round which they used to rally with such proud enthusiasm.

Far different is the state of public feeling in Germany. Ask a Prussian—not of that rank which makes the absence of any noble feeling a disgrace— but among those whose habits have not taught them the expediency of affecting such exalted sentiment, if they have it not—ask such a one his opinion of his country, her government, and her king; and you will be answered by such a hymn of love and praise, as might teach those, who have ears to hear, that passing a reform bill is not the most successful manner of securing the affection and applause of *the multitude.*

Chapter VI.

Journey to Cologne—Reasons for Travelling—The Cathedral—Museum—Public Walks — Music — Bonn —Concert—Students—Smoking.

We left Aix-la-Chapelle in a diligence, not having, at that time, fully mastered the problem, whether delay *plus* independence equalled in value despatch *minus* comfort. Our companions were a very agreeable old militaire commandant of Juliers; a young student, going, I believe, to the University of Bonn; and an elderly gentlewoman, who no sooner discovered me to be her countrywoman, than she appropriated me to herself, as her own particular listener; two young men, her nephews, were in another part of the vehicle, and she therefore appeared to be greatly in want of such a commodity. I was rather vexed at being thus constrained to give up hearing many amusing anecdotes, which our military companion was detailing: but as I found something very whimsical, though, perhaps, not very new, in the *projet de voyage* of my countrywoman, I soon gave her my undivided attention; and, having scribbled our conversation as soon as it was over, I will transcribe it for the benefit of my reader, who may be at a loss for a reason why it is good for him to travel.

"It is quite a pleasure," said the lady, "to meet an Englishwoman. I never speak anything but English. Pray, ma'am, is your journey to be a long or a short one?"

"As long as the summer will enable me to make it," I replied.

"Oh, then, I see that you travel quite in my way: you will go as far as possible within the time you can spare. My intention," she continued, "is to get as far as Geneva, and then to Paris.... How long may it be since you left London, ma'am?"

I answered that I believed it was about six weeks.

"Six weeks from London! Why we have done it in six days. What can have delayed you so long?"

I told her that we had met with many things which we were anxious to see.

"I think that is just the notion, begging your pardon, that prevents people from ever taking a really long journey in proportion to the time they are about it. I, and my nephews, make a point of never stopping to look at things."

"But does not such rapid travelling fatigue you?" said I.

"Oh, dear, no! am I not sitting still all the time? It is just so much rest—and that is exactly the reason I like travelling. Seeing sights would tire me to death—it always does in London; but driving along in this way is quite pleasant. No, no; nothing will ever induce me to tire myself by running after curiosities in every town I pass through: I make the greatest point of never seeing sights."

The commandant here drew my attention to some anecdote about Napoleon, and, for a few minutes, I was permitted to listen to him; but the lady then sought to renew our conversation, by asking if I was aware that the climate of Switzerland required great precaution.

"We have very little luggage," said she; "I am as particular about that, as about not seeing sights. My young men and I have each of us a cloak-bag—that is all I allow; but even in this I have contrived to pack an oil-skin hood and cloak, for stepping in and out of the stages. I should be sadly put out if I caught cold just in travelling through Switzerland."

This was certainly the *ne plus ultra* of travelling for travelling sake; but I afterwards encountered more than one party who appeared to proceed somewhat on the same principle.

The weather was beautifully clear the day we arrived at Cologne, and from our windows at the *Grosser Rheinberg* we first caught the wild outline of the *Siebengeberg*, or seven mountains. I have often heard these called the *Drachenfels*, why I know not, for that name belongs only to one of the seven; but be this as it may, these Drachenfels, or Siebengeberg, or seven mountains, form a most magnificent portal to the scenery of the Rhine; and when seen, for the first time, beyond the plain on which Cologne is situated, they set the imagination busily at work, to anticipate all the wonders behind them.

It was impossible to look upon the Rhine, and

upon the misty sevenfold grandeur of these hills, without longing instantly to embark, and be amongst them. But the city of the three Kings was not to be treated thus; and a second thought recalled not only the glories of Caspar Melchior and Balthasar, but also of the stupendous cathedral that sheltered their relics. We therefore determined upon devoting two days to the venerable city where Clovis was proclaimed king, and of which Pepin was duke before he ascended the throne of France.

Every quarter of Cologne is full of the highest historical interest; and, instead of two days, two months might be profitably spent in becoming acquainted with its antiquities: but as long as steamboats keep running up the Rhine, the giddy throng, who come flying over sea and land to look at its rocks and its ruins, will never spare time to examine this interesting old city with one tenth part of the attention it deserves.

The day after our arrival was, most fortunately for us, a Sunday; and we enjoyed a treat which, I will venture to say, no one can form the slightest idea of, if they have not themselves tasted it. It is difficult to speak of the *Münster Church* of Cologne, without employing words which would to many appear greatly misplaced, when applied to a building not more than half completed. Were I to say, for instance, that the most exalted imagination could conceive nothing more perfect in Teutonic architecture, it might perhaps be asked, if I considered deal planks as the perfection of Gothic roofing; and if I confessed that the impression made upon my mind was more like the effect of magic than of reality, I might hear that a tower half-reared, and surmounted by a hideous crane, could be obtained without the aid of necromancy. Nevertheless, in both cases, I should speak the truth. I can never forget, nor perhaps ever again hope to enjoy, the exceeding delight I experienced from hearing high mass performed in the choir of this matchless church. The graceful windows, each one a separate wonder, rearing their bold and light proportions to the towering roof, let in such streams of gorgeous-coloured light, that the whole edifice glowed with it.

The service was performed with great solemnity

and pomp: the music, consisting of an organ, and very fine string accompaniments, was most glorious; and the voices, rich, firm, and in perfect harmony, made us feel that we were indeed in Germany. In addition to all this, delicious incense rolled its sweet cloud of fragrance over our heads, and completed the enchantment. This beautiful choir is lined behind the stalls with tapestry, from designs by Rubens: it is so wretchedly faded as to render the subjects nearly unintelligible; but were they as fresh as in the hour when the needle finished its unprofitable labour, and had they been designed by Raphael, or Apelles himself, they would still be most miserably ill-placed where they are. What decoration of the kind could look otherwise than pitiful, under a vault rising one hundred and fifty feet from the earth, on pillars so boldly majestic, that they branch into arches for its support, apparently only a few feet from its summit?

The miserable organ-loft, too, would be painfully felt to disfigure the sublimity of the building, were it not that the eye naturally rises to the immense space above, so rich in beauty from every source that can give splendour and nobleness to a church; and the puny work of yesterday is forgotten.

It was not till after long and repeated visits to this wonderful building, that we recollected the absolute necessity of seeing the celebrated treasures it contains in gems and relics: these are said to be immense in value—and so in truth they ought to be, in proportion to the extravagant sum asked for showing them, which is no less than fifteen francs. I believe I should have demurred at this demand, had not another party proposed to divide the fee with us. This arrangement being settled, we began to look, to wonder, and to admire, as ivory, gold, and precious stones were displayed before us. But the wonder of wonders is the Mausoleum of the Eastern Kings: with the most grave and dignified assumption of historical truth, you are informed that this splendid monument contains not only the bones of Caspar Melchior and Balthasar, but likewise those of St. Felix, St. Nabor, and St. Gregory.

Let the bones contained in it be whose they may,

the shrine itself is most superb; and when you enter the little tabernacle in which it is deposited, there is something so mystically glowing in the eternal lamplight reflected by the gold and precious stones —something so horrific in the three grim skulls, protruding themselves from amidst the jewels with which they are encircled, for each one,

" The likeness of a kingly crown has on,"

and the whole scene is at once so ghastly, and so gorgeous, that, for the moment, one is almost tempted to believe that some real sanctity must be attached to the relics, which princes and prelates have for ages agreed to honour with such extravagant and strange devotion. The date of this singular monument is 1170.

It is said that the King of Prussia is extremely desirous to finish, or at least to proceed with this splendid edifice: but, hitherto, all the money devoted to it has but sufficed to carry on the costly, but most necessary, repairs. The foundations of the church are of basalt; but, unfortunately, the superstructure is of the crumbling stone of the Drachenfels, and the work of the elements is sadly visible upon it. Workmen are at present employed in covering the whole external surface with some unctuous composition, which, it is hoped, will preserve it from further injury; the colour of this is so nearly that of the stone itself, that when perfectly dry, it will not, I think, disfigure it.

There is an admirable picture by Rubens in the church of St. Peter: it represents the terrible crucifixion of that saint, and I could hardly have believed, unless I had felt it, how completely the influence of a powerful genius can overcome disgust and horror. Hideous as is the subject of this picture, it is impossible to look at it without delight. Rubens was christened in this church; and the house in which he was born, distinguished by his portrait hanging over the door, is at no great distance from it.

The Musée de Wallrof has many curious old pictures, and a very interesting collection of local Roman antiquities. The rooms containing them were exceedingly crowded when we made our visit; so much so, indeed, as to make the passing from one to another a matter of considerable difficulty.

We entered it on Sunday, immediately after the cathedral service, and found much interest and amusement in examining the appearance of the mixed assemblage which filled the rooms. The dresses in general were perhaps more picturesque than elegant; the *endimanchés* of the city, indeed, were many of them exceedingly well dressed; but the majority of the company had the appearance of peasants in their holiday attire; and the highly-finished, but uncouth groups in violet and in green, which adorned the walls, though many of them stood forth from a background of gold, were hardly more gaudy in colouring, or grotesque in outline, than some of the parties who came to visit them.

The public walks and drives round the town, though seen to great disadvantage immediately after the beautiful promenades of Aix-la-Chapelle, are very pretty, and almost every part of the city affords picturesque and interesting points of view. On crossing the bridge of boats to Deutz, the scene is peculiarly striking; the whole city, with all its variety of venerable towers, is spread out before the eye, and with the river for its foreground, forms a most magnificent picture.

That peculiar national characteristic of Germany—a love of music, with the almost universal advantages of voice and ear, are strongly manifested at Cologne. At our table-d'hôte we had a violin concerto, which many a London soirée would have gladly welcomed; and the mere accidental warblings in the street which reached me through my chamber windows, were of a tone and cadence very unlike any sounds I had been accustomed so to hear.

Much as I wished to find myself fairly launched on the Rhine, I regretted not having more time to devote to Cologne; and as it was a city of vows, I registered something very like one in my memory, that I would not leave the country without making it a second visit.

On the 8th of July we left this city of the kings for Bonn, by the Prince Frederick steam-boat; but, though greatly delighted by the consciousness of being actually floating on that " abounding river," which has formed the theme of so much enthusiastic admiration, it was impossible to deny that its banks were, at this portion of it, as devoid of beauty as well could be. The Seven Hills, however, seemed to beckon us on, and to promise all that was wanting to give interest to a stream, which, in the copious volume and immense rapidity of its waters, yields to so few of the rivers of Europe. Excepting the gradual approach to these hills, there was nothing in this little voyage to atone to me for leaving Cologne so hastily: but on reaching Bonn, I found enough to convince me that I was travelling through a country where I should find small leisure to lament the objects I had passed, amid the busy interest excited by those I had reached.

If Bonn had nothing but its University, this would be sufficient to detain the traveller very delightfully for several days; but there are many other circumstances to repay such a delay It is full of interesting antiquities, and it has the charm of being the first point at which one's expectations of beautiful scenery begin to be realised. There are views in the environs of Bonn equal in extent and richness to almost anything on the Rhine.

This very pretty town was formerly an electoral

residence, and the palace, which is an extensive and handsome building, at present makes part of the University. Everything connected with the University is upon a noble scale : the schools, the library, the academic walks, and gardens are all handsome, and arranged in a grand and expensive style. To those who have their fancies over full of the Gothic glories of Oxford, or imagine that on any other spot of earth they shall meet the perfection of King's College Chapel, or the magnificence of Trinity College at Cambridge, Bonn may cause a sensation of disappointment : but to all who are sufficiently instructed to be aware that the academic magnificence of England stands alone, it will appear what it really is,—a noble and beautiful seat of learning.

The bronze statue of the Empress Helen, the sainted mother of Constantine, is the most interesting object in the cathedral, which has been too much defaced by repairs to retain any great claim to admiration.

The walk on the Altezoll should by no means be neglected: both from thence and from the gardens behind the café, strangely styled *Vinea Domini*, the view is delightful.

The musical reputation of Bonn is considerable: it boasts Beethoven among its élèves; and during the reign and residence of the last elector, some of the first performers of the age made it their headquarters. Perhaps it was this reputation, though belonging rather to the past than to the present times, which induced us to give three hours of a lovely summer's evening to a public concert given by a Madame Milden. The sacrifice, for such I certainly felt it, was, however, not in vain, the whole scene being new and amusing. The apartment used for this occasion was the ball-room, about one-fourth of which was occupied by the orchestra; but without any other line of division than a clear space between the last bench occupied by the company and the first music-stands. We were told that there were between three and four hundred people present.

I was extremely pleased to find myself in a room so well filled with German company; at a point sufficiently distant from any metropolis to enable me to judge of the national style, when divested of that conventional air and tone which have made almost all characteristic national varieties disappear in the great cities of Europe. This must inevitably be the case, whenever people agree to submit themselves to the uniform laws of high breeding and cultivated taste: but at Bonn this livery of elegance was neither to be hoped nor feared; and I found as many points of difference between Madame Milden's concert, and all other assemblies of the same kind that I had seen elsewhere, as I could possibly wish. Yet there was nothing in the slightest degree displeasing or uncouth. The extreme simplicity of dress was the first thing which struck me, while reviewing the female part of the company; but a few moments' prolonged examination of the faces around which the luxuriant tresses were so simply braided, sufficed to convince me that the fair girls were right to trust more to their blooming complexions, and sweet expression of countenance, than to a more elaborate toilet: we remarked many extremely lovely faces among them.

After the room appeared to be perfectly full, a door, which I had not before remarked, opened to admit a party, some of whom had a very decided air of metropolitan *bon ton*. They placed themselves on chairs, on one side of the foremost bench, and the performance immediately began.

A fair neighbour, who appeared very willing to converse with me, announced their names and titles; but I forget both: I think she said that they resided in the neighbourhood. One of the party was as lovely and graceful a woman as I ever saw. This distinguished set was immediately surrounded by a party of officers: on the broad chest of one of these I counted seven decorations.

The orchestra was very respectably filled, and one violin concerto excellent. Madame Milden sung three or four songs in good style, and with a powerful voice, which had, however, seen better days; but she was enthusiastically applauded; and, when not singing, placed herself among the company, many of whom, particularly the *élite*, conversed with her with an air of great affability and kindness.

Of course no public meeting can take place at Bonn in which the young students do not make a distinguished figure. On this occasion they did not appear to mix much with the company, but stood almost entirely apart in groups of three or four, and forming pictures, which made me fancy myself in a saloon with Vandyke and Rubens; for certainly such must have been their models.

I suppose it is in the nature of all young gentlemen, particularly when congregated together, to mix a little fancy, and perhaps *tant soit peu* of affectation in their outward seeming. Something of this may assuredly be seen both at Oxford and Cambridge, despite the gown and cap which so greatly curb the display of individual whim: but at Bonn, where no academic dress is worn, the costume of the young men is sometimes marvellously imaginative.

Whenever a set of European youths assemble to receive the last finish of their education, it is probable that some will always be found among them upon whom the stamp which marks the gentleman is too strongly impressed to permit any vagary of dress to conceal it; and of such many are to be seen among the students of Bonn; but the majority are much more picturesque.

Hair, long and exquisitely dishevelled; throats bare, with collars turned back almost to the shoulders; with here a miniature beard, curiously trimmed into a perfect triangle; and there moustaches, long, thin, and carefully curled, might be seen repeated in one knot after another, through the whole length of the room. Some presented a fair young forehead bared à la Byron, and others looked about them with a wild eye rolling à la Juan. One had the pale cheek and deep-set eye of a premature philosopher; while another looked with such a dashing, reckless sauciness upon all around, that I felt inclined to watch him, half from fear, and half from fun, to see what mad-cap frolic would deliver him of the load of merry mischief that lay laughing in his eye.

Not the slightest indecorum, however, to the amount even of a too audible whisper, disturbed the entertainment; and, notwithstanding all we hear of the boisterous licence assumed by the students of Germany, I question if so large a party of young men could often be seen assembled, and remain as long together, so entirely without noise or disturbance of any kind.

L'hôtel de Cologne, where we had taken up our abode, was far from uncomfortable, though situated in a street so extremely narrow, as to render a sitting-room which was exactly opposite the one we occupied rather nearer than we might have wished. It was inhabited by a young officer, upon whose retirement I would certainly not have permitted my eyes to intrude, had his mode of passing his morning permitted me to avoid it: but his two large windows being opened from the top to the bottom of the room, he took his coffee as much in public as if he had been on a stage; and by no device, except sitting in total darkness, could we avoid seeing him. Such being the case, we submitted to the necessity; and certainly were not a little amused by the scene that passed before our eyes. On one side of his room hung a row of splendid pipes, amounting, I should think, to nearly a dozen : having dismissed his coffee, he selected one of these, and placing himself at the window, soon became enveloped in an atmosphere, the mysterious charm of which none, I suppose, but a German can fully understand. The countenance of our military neighbour expressed all that tranquil serenity which one is sure to find on all features seen athwart a cloud of tobacco-smoke: but after a time the ample bowl became exhausted, and something like weariness seemed to mix itself with the supine beatitude he was enjoying. He placed his prodigious hookah against the window-frame, stretched his legs, and yawned.

Ere long, however, the door opened, and a gentleman entered, whom he welcomed with the most cordial satisfaction: but the next moment, nay, the very same in which he grasped his hand in friendly greeting, he flew to his collection of pipes, and selecting the largest among them, put it into the hands of his friend. He then hastened to replenish his own, which being done, they both sat down together at the open window with every appearance of enjoyment, and in a few moments the mutual vapour hid them from our sight. This is a species of social pleasure which it is very difficult for the uninitiated to appreciate: we can only darkly guess its value, by weighing all that is sacrificed to obtain it.

Chapter VII.

Godesberg—The Seven Hills—Drachenfels—Friesdorf — Stromberg — Catholic Devotion — Kreutzberg — Buried Monks—Table-d'hôte—German Manners—Unkel—Laacher-see.

Having given as much time as we could spare to Bonn, we left it in one of the pleasant, but queer-looking open carriages of the country, and proceeded to Godesberg, a small village at the distance of a league and a half, where several of my Rhine-travelled friends had desired us to halt, for the purpose of enjoying at leisure the first perfect specimen of Rhenish scenery.

We have every reason to thank them for their counsel, for the week we passed there was delightful: yet I doubt if, merely considering the locality, Godesberg be as favourable a position, as head-quarters for the tourist, as some other places farther up the river. It has, however, many advantages, which perhaps no other village can boast:

the accommodations are everything that the most fastidious traveller could desire; and it rarely happens during the summer months that he fails to meet with agreeable society, who, coming there, like himself, for the purpose of enjoyment, are just in the frame of mind to seek amusement from every source within their reach; and the conversation at the table-d'hôte is more like that of a private party than of chance-met stranger wanderers.

There are two excellent hotels in the village. We had been directed to Blinker's, which is much the largest establishment; but here not an inch of room could be obtained, and we then addressed ourselves to the Belle-vue, or, as it is translated on the cards, the " Beautiful Sight;" and this we found so exceedingly commodious, and the party assembled there so very agreeable, that we ceased not to rejoice at the chance which had thrown us into such excellent quarters.

I should write a volume upon Godesberg, were I to indulge myself in speaking at length of its walks, its donkey rides, its ruins, its dilapidated nunnery, its mineral spring, and its easy, amiable sociability.

But it might, perhaps, be pleasanter to write than to read; and as people will drive up the Rhine as fast as steam can carry them, and down again with all the swiftness of the stream to boot, it matters little for them to hear of pleasures which it enters not into their projects to share.

The valley of the Rhine, which begins at Bingen, ends at Kœnigswinter, a pretty rambling village lying at the feet of the Seven Mountains, and immediately opposite to Godesberg. One of our first excursions was to this place. We crossed the river in a little boat, which hardly seems to have business enough to entitle it to the name of ferry-boat, but which we always found ready to take us the moment we reached the bank. The greatest drawback to the delights of Godesberg is its distance from this bank: it is more than a mile; and when you pitch your tent expressly for the purpose of enjoying the Rhine, it is a serious evil to have a mile to traverse before you reach it.

At Kœnigswinter we readily found donkeys, and a guide to lead us to the summit of the Drachenfels. This seems to be the favourite of the Seven Mountains: at least it appeared to me that every one I conversed with respecting this region had scaled its rocky side; though very few had taken the trouble of mounting any of the others. This may partly be owing to its popular name, which is familiar to every one, while those of the Wolkenberg, Stromberg, Lowenberg, Niederberg, Oelberg, and Hemmerich, are only mentioned occasionally, to prove one's superior local knowledge. Another reason for undertaking the toilsome ascent of the Drachenfels is the ruin which stands so boldly on its very apex; and another still is the legend of the Dragon, whose cavern is shown in its side. There are several stations on the road up this steep ascent, where my patient and well-tutored beast permitted us to pause, and to look up and down the Rhine. The views *almost* realized all I had dreamed of its beauty. When we reached the top, I found the precipice, that fell directly from the foot of the ruined castle, so fearfully abrupt, that I hardly dared to stand upon its giddy edge while the guide pointed out the objects below. The front of this precipitous rock has been worked into as a quarry;

at least, such is the tradition; though the hollow, pointed out as the spot from whence the stones were taken, is so high in air as to render the statement almost incredible to me, particularly as the same stone might have been obtained below: but my doubts are quite unsupported by any authority.

This bold attack upon Nature is said to have been made by Archbishop Conrad, in 1284, for the purpose of building the cathedral of Cologne; and this point of the mountain is called the Domquarry. Another object at which we were bid to look was a yawning cavern, which opened its black portal in a hollow on the opposite side of the little ravine over which we hung. This mysterious-looking chasm is called the Dombruch; and the man very gravely assured us, that it was the home of the celebrated dragon who had given his name to the mountain on which we stood. Exactly overlooking the abode of this ominous neighbour, stands the castle, whose origin is so remote as to be lost in fable. Some portion of the beetling rock on which it stands has been rent away; and the ruin now literally hangs over the precipice, one corner of it projecting several feet beyond any support whatever. The view from this point is prodigiously grand; and all the features of the spot are wild and impressive in the extreme. On the very summit of the mountain, and there only, Henry discovered an enormous block of lava; which, in conjunction with the crater-like form of the Wolkenberg, just below it, made us feel that we were in a region which had been visited by some violent convulsion of Nature.

While we were enjoying all this in perfect silence, our guide suddenly thought proper to awaken the celebrated echo of the Siebengeberg, by some of the most hideous noises that the voice of man ever produced. If such sounds be often heard, repeated from rock to rock, and from mountain to mountain, it is not wonderful that this castle peak has the reputation of being haunted; for never did more unearthly notes strike upon the ear than those our Caliban of a guide produced. He laughed, he shrieked, he bellowed, till the dragon himself might have trembled to hear him.

On descending from the mountain, which we did on the side farthest from the river, we had a singular and beautiful view over the wavy tops of the innumerable hills, from among which the Siebengeberg rise. It was, I confess, in this direction only that I could perceive any portion of that sublimity which I had heard so lavishly attributed to the region of the Drachenfels. The Oelberg, which, I believe, is the highest, rises only 1827 feet above the level of the river; and though they form altogether a very noble feature in a very beautiful landscape, I cannot think they merit the epithet of sublime. But this vast extent of pine-covered heights, with the dark and intricate valleys, which wind along them, the frequent bare masses of rock, protruding their capricious forms, and looking like the giant inhabitants of the woods, added to the seven bolder heights that raise their crested heads above them all, form together a scene so wild, so desolate, as may well justify the use of such a term.

It is only during a part of the descent, however, that this is enjoyed; the road winds round the side of the mountain, and ere long brought us in sight of a landscape, forming as perfect a contrast to it as it is well possible to imagine. The splendid river rolled its vast mass of waters at our feet: below us hung terrace after terrace of vines, just swelling with the promise of an abundant vintage: while, on the opposite bank, such fields of yellow corn were spread out before us, as might have made Ceres herself laugh to look upon them. Never, I think, did so short a space divide scenes so utterly discordant.

After recrossing the river, we took a path through the fields, which led us by a short cut to Godesberg. The fine ruins of its castle were exactly before us, and we saw the sun set behind them in a style of unusual splendour. The whole mass seemed on fire; for the rich red light streamed through every crevice of the ruined wall, and appeared to wrap round the base of the isolated tower, making it look much smaller at bottom than at top: the effect of this delusion was most singular.

How keenly we enjoyed our delicious coffee after this long expedition! The fair hands of Mademoiselle (for thus only was our active little landlady ever designated) prepared it; and the assiduous attention with which she performed every service of the kind most assuredly deserves to be recorded in recommendation of the " Beautiful Sight." Notwithstanding there were waiters and chambermaids in abundance, this kind-hearted little lady seemed to mix her own thoughtful care with every service they performed; and one felt certain that it was only necessary to make "*Mademoiselle*" acquainted with a wish or a want, to have it supplied promptly, cheerfully, and effectually.

The next day we set out upon an exploring walk, Mr. H. with his pencil, and Henry with his hammer. After lingering for awhile among the beautiful ruins of Godesberg, we turned to the left, and passed through fields profuse in their promises of bread and wine, till we reached the wood that covers the whole range of hills from Godesberg to Bonn. Here we soon fell into a gravel path, so pleasant to the feet, and so abounding in pretty points from which to look out upon the river below, that we were led on by the mere pleasure of walking, without any definite object in view, for a distance that we afterwards learned was nearly four miles.

At length we reached an open space, where the wood, and indeed every trace of vegetation, suddenly ceased; and we saw an enormous mine before us, in and about which a vast number of workmen were employed. We soon found that we had blindly stumbled upon a most interesting spot —no other than the extensive brown-coal deposit of Friesdorf. Even the most ignorant eye cannot examine this singular formation with indifference; and I am tempted to transcribe a note from my son's journal, which, I think, describes it more intelligibly than I can do.

"The stratum contains large masses of wood in every stage, from simple wood, to stone, or iron ore, which still retain all the marks of organization. The superior stratum of this range of hills is gravel: under this there is a stiff, blue, sandy clay, which is used in a neighbouring pottery. This has thin layers of the brown coal in it, and likewise detached masses of wood, together with sulphuret of iron mineralizing the smaller branches. Beneath this is the first stratum of brown coal, about five feet thick, or rather more in some places; under this is the alum earth, sufficient in quantity to employ some considerable alum works erected close to the excavation. I have collected several good specimens of the fossil wood, in all its different stages—one of them, a stem embedded in the iron ore, is extremely beautiful. The fossil remains of several kinds of fishes, and a very few fresh-water shells, have also been found here, from which there is great reason to believe this brown coal formation to be a lacustrine deposit. I am told that some trunks of trees have been found of thirty feet in circumference, and that all lie in an east and-west direction.

"The stratum of alum-earth, beneath the brown coal, is of a dark purple or almost black colour, and very unctuous to the touch: there are crystals of the alum in the small fissures of the clay, of a very pure white, but exceedingly minute. This stratum is also about five feet thick, and beneath it is another of the brown coal of nine feet. Under this is white clay, which, I am told, has been bored to the depth of sixty feet, without coming to its termination."

After passing above an hour in examining what looked like the relics of a buried forest, we proceeded to visit the alum works and the pottery. A great number of men were employed in each; and both here, and among the much larger number engaged in the different processes of the brown coal works, we were struck with the respectful and unobtrusive civility of the labourers. When they observed us engaged in examining the fragments of disinterred wood which were lying about, many of them came round us with specimens; but the moment they had put them into our hands they retired, without showing the least indication of expecting to be paid for them.

The following morning we again crossed the Rhine to Kœnigswinter, when I once more mounted the obedient donkey who had done me such good service on my former expedition, and, attended by my two squires, prepared to mount the Stromberg. Nothing can be much less interesting than the road which leads to its summit, for it is cut through a wood so thickly grown, that a high, dark vegetable wall is all you can see on either side. The ascent is not so steep as that of the Drachenfels, but much longer, and I was heartily tired before I reached the top. Here we hoped to be rewarded for our tedious climbing; but found the trees too high in every direction to permit our seeing anything on earth but themselves, and the singular little church dedicated to St. Peter, which crowns the very summit of the mountain. It is said that this almost inaccessible chapel was built by a knight, named Diether, in consequence of a vow made in Palestine. This story is rendered probable by the impossibility of supposing that any one, not bound by a vow, would have selected such a spot for the purpose. A small shanty for the sale of *schnaps*, milk, and black bread, to restore the strength of any pious pilgrims who may reach it, is now the only human habitation on the Stromberg.

It is recorded, however, that in days of yore sundry holy hermits made it their abode: if so, these self-denying anchorites might truly be said to have been above temptation; and, as they proved themselves *quite unfit* for earth and its blessings, by choosing the dank hollows of this dismal mountain to dwell in, instead of the rich and smiling valley at its foot, let us hope they were *more fit* for heaven.

We descended by a different path from that which led us up, and again enjoyed a view over the dark, dreamy region which we saw when coming down the Drachenfels. Nevertheless, mounting the Stromberg, or Petersberg, as it is often called, is an exploit, which I would recommend to no traveller, who has not a positive pleasure in the act of climbing, independently of any object to be attained by it. It is certain, however, that this mountain, uninteresting as it appears at present, must have been held in much religious reverence; for we counted no less than fifty-six crosses, or stations, as they are called, on its side. Many of these have evidently been lately repaired, and still more have the marks of recent devotion; for we saw many flowers, not yet completely faded, either lying at the feet of the Saviour, or adorning the brows of his mother.

A proof of this feeling was given by the lad who acted as our guide. As I preferred walking to riding down the descent, I dismissed him with the donkey soon after we reached the top. As we returned, following in the path he had taken, we observed a bright fresh wreath of beech-leaves twisted round the bust of a wooden Virgin, while evident traces of my donkey's hoofs were visible upon the side of the little hillock, on which she was stationed.

There is something to me extremely pleasing in these outward and visible signs of religious feeling, especially when demonstrated where no human eye is expected to approve it : nor can they, I think, be classed with those superstitious observances with which the Roman Catholic religion has been so reasonably reproached.

Another day of our stay at Godesberg, or, at least, the morning of it, was spent in visiting Kreutzberg, a high and very singular hill near Bonn. The road which led to it passed through Poppelsdorf, where some handsome buildings connected with the University of Bonn are situated. Every feature in the scenery of this village is beautiful, and the road that leads to the top of Mount Calvary, or Kreutzberg, magnificent.

The isolated building that stands on the summit of this hill was formerly a convent of Servites; it is surrounded by an ample garden, and commands one of the finest views in the neighbourhood. At present it appears to be occupied solely by peasants; and the only trace left of this once celebrated establishment is the church, which is still considered as an edifice of peculiar sanctity. All travellers are sent to this spot, both to see the wondrous chapel, and to look upon the long-interred, but still undecayed bodies of the monks, which lie in a vault beneath it.

We met here, as indeed happened to us in many other points of our wanderings, a very agreeable party of Dutch travellers, who, like ourselves, were come to look at the wonders of the place. The rencontre was particularly fortunate upon this occasion, as we had long to wait before the guardian of the tomb returned from an excursion he was making in the neighbourhood. Meantime, however, we had the church to see. Having sufficiently examined its various altars and antique monuments, we were led, by a narrow staircase behind the high altar, to a small chamber above. As there was nothing whatever in this room to gratify curiosity, its only decorations being a few copes and surplices hanging upon the walls, we were at a loss to guess why we were brought there; but after a few moments' delay, our conductor opened a door, and led us from the dark obscure room in which we stood, into a chapel extremely rich in its decoration, but of most singular form and arrangement. The entire width of the building (between thirty and forty feet) is occupied by a magnificent flight of stairs, divided into three compartments. The centre one, which occupies about half of the entire space, is of superb Italian marble; this is fenced on each side by a handsome double balustrade, dividing it from the inferior staircases which flank it, and which reach to the outer wall of the building; at the top of the marble stair is an altar, with a large figure of the Saviour suspended over it.

The door by which we entered was on a level with this altar; and having stepped to the front of it, I was about to descend the marble flight, when our conductor seized my arm, and exclaimed in

French, with much vehemence, "These stairs are sacred!"

I apologized for my indecorous attempt, by stating my ignorance of their history: the offence, I imagine, is not an uncommon one among the numerous heretic travellers who visit the shrine, for he readily accepted the excuse; and proceeded to inform us, that three drops of the Saviour's blood rest upon these holy stones. "They fell," he said, "from the wounds the thorns had made, and dropped on the steps which led to the judgment-seat of Pilate." The morsels of stone which received them are inserted on three of the marble stairs, and are covered by thin plates of gold. This relic, together with the sumptuous marble in which it is lodged, was a gift from one of the Archbishops of Cologne to the monastery of Kreutzberg; accompanied by a bull from the Pope, which hangs near the entrance to the chapel, announcing to all pilgrims, who may visit the holy spot, that it is sacrilege to place a foot upon the centre stairs (except for an armed knight, whose armour would prevent him from using his knees); but that to mount them kneeling, ensures plenary indulgence for a year.

The form of the ceiling is very graceful, and ornamented with fresco painting. On the floor of the building, immediately at the foot of the stairs, are a pair of enormous folding doors, which open upon the forest; through these, in more Catholic times, vast numbers of pilgrims used to pour at particular seasons of the year to perform this act of devotion.

Beneath this chapel is a subterranean chamber, representing the stable, and all the accompaniments of the nativity. Among the numerous plaster figures which occupy the scene, we recognised our friends Caspar, Melchior, and Balthasar, in the act of presenting their gifts. Everything about this singular place seems to mark the very extremity of superstitious devotion.

The examination of all this took more than an hour; but still the sacristan had not returned. The Dutch party, as well as ourselves, were desirous to wait for him; for it was, in fact, the sight he had to show, which had brought us there: so we walked in the garden, we climbed the tower, we ate cherries, we read every inscription in the church, yet still he came not. At length, much fatigued, but, nevertheless, steadfast in our determination to wait for him, we all assembled round the high altar, near which was the large trap-door that opened upon the vault; and having seated ourselves upon the steps and benches round it, endeavoured to beguile by conversation the still prolonged absence of the sacristan.

I remarked on this occasion, and, in truth, on every other that gave me an opportunity of conversing with them, that the Dutch are not only extremely courteous in their manner to strangers, but that they are particularly well-informed and intelligent. After this observation, it will appear like national vanity if I say that they resemble the English: but they certainly do so, in their passion for travelling; and in the active perseverance of their researches for information. I do not, however, claim these remarks as my own: they were made to me by a German of high rank, who knew both countries well. He added, that the English and Dutch were often mistaken for each other at the German inns: " but this," said he, "probably arises from the wealth and indifference to expense so remarkable in both."

At length the person we were all so anxiously awaiting, entered the church. I hardly know what we had expected from this sepulchral examination; but it certainly must have been something very different from the reality; for we were jesting and laughing when the man arrived: and even when we saw the two lads, who accompanied him, raise the massy door, I believe not one of us felt any portion of the awe which the scene it opened to us was calculated to inspire. The sacristan, with a lighted candle in his hand, descended a dark and narrow flight of steps, desiring us to follow him: I was the first that did so: and I shall not soon forget the spectacle that met my eyes. On each side of us, as we entered the vault, was ranged a row of open coffins, each containing the dry and shrivelled body of a monk, in his robe and cowl. They are so placed as to be exposed to the closest examination both of touch and sight; and the remembrance of my walk through them still makes me shudder.

The wonderful state of preservation in which these bodies remain, though constantly exposed to the atmosphere by being thus exhibited, is attributed by good Catholics to the peculiar sanctity of the place : but to those who do not receive this solution of the mystery, it is one of great difficulty. The dates of their interment vary from 1400 to 1713; and the oldest is quite as fresh as the most recent. There are twenty-six, fully exposed to view; and apparently many more beneath them. From the older ones, the coffins have either crumbled away, or the bodies were buried without them. In some of these ghastly objects the flesh is still full, and almost shapely upon the legs; in others it appears to be drying gradually away, and the bones are here and there becoming visible. The condition of the face also varies very greatly, though by no means in proportion to the antiquity of each. In many, the nose, lips, and beard remain; and in one, the features were so little disturbed, that

"All unruffled was his face,
We trusted his soul had gotten grace."

Round others, the dust lies where it had fallen, as it dropped, grain by grain, from the mouldering cheeks; and the head grins from beneath the cowl nearly in the state of a skeleton. The garments are almost in the same unequal degree of preservation: for, in many the white material is still firm, though discoloured; while in others it is dropping away in fragments. The shoes of all are wonderfully perfect.

The last person buried in this vault was one who acted as gardener to the community. His head is crowned with a wreath of flowers, which still preserves its general form: nay, the larger blossoms may yet be distinguished from the smaller ones; but the withered leaves lie mixed with his fallen hair on either side.

Altogether the scene is well calculated to produce a cold shiver in the beholder; and yet we all lingered over it. There is certainly some nerve within us, that thrills with strange pleasure at the touch of horror.

Our long delay at Kreutzberg prevented our return to the hotel in time for the table-d'hôte; nd though sufficiently fatigued to render a lazy, lounging meal very agreeable, we had begun to find so much charm in the society, that we much regretted losing it on this occasion; and the more so, as the time drew near when we must lose it probably for ever. While recalling the party, which we found on arriving at Godesberg, and which continued together as long as we remained, I am tempted to give a slight sketch of the principal members of it; chiefly for the benefit of such of my countrymen, and countrywomen, as may be fearful of speaking at a public table when travelling, lest their words should fall on ears not sufficiently refined to be worthy of receiving them. This shrinking kind of aristocracy is worse than needless when travelling in Germany; and I believe it occasions to those who yield to it, the loss of half the pleasure their travels might afford.

Should these pages reach any of the party to whom I allude, and should they recognise the portraits, I trust they will forgive the freedom, as it goes not the length of affixing names; and will accept the record as a proof of the pleasing remembrance I cherish of them.

At the head of the table was the Dowager Baroness * * * * *, of one of the noblest houses in Germany. Short as was my acquaintance with this lady, I could not fail to perceive that she was a person of no common endowments; full of spirited and original observation, and gifted with that enviable species of wit which makes even an ordinary thought seem striking. She never spoke without winning all within reach of her to listen.

On her left hand sat Count * * * *, a very distinguished Belgian officer, of the old régime, who was on the Duke of Wellington's staff at Waterloo: on her right, his lovely, graceful, and most fascinating Countess. This charming woman was more like the *beau ideal* of a fabled heroine, than any person I ever saw. Were I to follow such a being as Madame d'Arblay's Cecilia into married life I should fancy her just such another. I have often watched the Countess * * * * in the garden before our hotel, surrounded by her four children; almost too beautiful and light in figure to be supposed their mother; yet too watchful of their sports, and too tender in her caresses, to be mistaken for any other. It was a real benefit to have one's path crossed by such a vision. The recollections of her voice, her look, and her manner form a portrait which will hang for ever in that division of memory where we turn to look for what is beautiful and good.

Near the Countess sat a young lady, to whose conversation I listened during the first day with much attention, in order to discover of what country she might be; but I totally failed, having left the table with the persuasion that she was a very clever Englishwoman. She spoke French, German, and English with equal facility; and conversed with the greatest vivacity in each, with different members of the party. She was unmarried, but a baroness in rank; and to my great surprise, I found that, instead of being English, she was Dutch.

Near her were placed an English officer of rank, and his wife. Were I to draw their portraits, it would be done with all the partiality of friendship, and I might get reproached for being *too English;* for we had afterwards the happiness of meeting them again more than once in the course of our journey; and the acquaintance thus casually begun will prove, I trust, as lasting as it was delightful.

Several other ladies, and one or two gentlemen, were occasionally added to the party, but they passed off too quickly to become much known to any of us. I must not, however, omit to mention two very young ladies, who remained all the time we stayed; one of them was an invalid, and came there to take the mineral waters of Draitsch. I never saw anything more sweetly refined and delicate than the demeanour of these young girls. They were quite by themselves; and the simple, unaffected, gentle reserve of their manner was quite beautiful. It was perhaps partly to avoid the attention, which it was evidently their wish to shun, that their dress was so very simple, as to make it impossible to judge their station by it. Had not a very handsome equipage frequently awaited their orders, I confess that, in my insular barbarism, I might have doubted their claims to the rank they really held. It is certain, I believe, that the Germans do not measure their own importance, or that of their neighbours and friends, by the style and value of their garments, so much as most other people do. They are often extremely well-dressed, but the general simplicity of their toilet is remarkable; and at the churches, the theatres, the public walks, or any other place of general resort, it is by the graceful salute, the delicate hand, or the softly-modulated voice, that the noble lady is distinguished; and not by her lawns and her lace.

My inquiries respecting these two young persons elicited another trait of national manners strikingly peculiar. One of them was the daughter of a gentleman of fortune in the neighbourhood, and the other her friend. They had neither of them a mother; and as it was thought that the health of one of them would be benefited by the waters of Draitsch, no more idea of difficulty or indecorum was attached to their taking up their abode at Godesberg for the purpose of drinking them, than if they had been young men instead of young women. I cannot pretend to judge what the morality of Germany may be; but I had frequent opportunities of remarking that the delicacy of female manners is preserved in the greatest perfection.

I have seldom witnessed a prettier gala scene than Godesberg offered on the Sunday that we passed there. The two hotels stand side by side, though not close together; and on the opposite side of the road are the large gardens which belong to them. These are not very carefully cultivated, being without any fence from the road; but they have shady walks and abundance of chairs and benches, whereon lovers of the open air may indulge in reading, meditating, or looking at the cheerful moving scene in front of the hotels. Large groups of donkeys, gay in their scarlet housings, stand ever ready to be mounted before the doors; and large parties of pedestrians often make a promenade there. But on Sunday all this is multiplied tenfold. Carriages from Bonn, and many of the neighbouring villages, come thronging in, filled with happy beings, intent upon a summer day's enjoyment; while gigs and sociables of every possible variety, crammed with the students of Poppelsdorf and Bonn, rattle past and through them with all the desperate gaiety of boyish frolic.

On these occasions the tables-d'hôte are doubled

and trebled; and the enjoyment of conversation is exchanged for that of seeing a very large party very particularly jovial. But the most pleasing scene is in the evening; when tables are placed in the open air for the coffee, wine, and fruit, which concludes the feasting of the day. The ladies throw their bonnets aside, leaving their fair faces no other protection but their beautiful and abundant hair. The gentlemen, many of them military, sit near, if a chair can be found: or if not, stand behind them like courteous cavaliers as they are; excepting when (oh, horror of horrors!) they turn aside from the lovely group, and smoke! Were it not for this most hateful practice, I should say that everything I saw of the social habits of Germany was delightful; but this is a stain which sadly disfigures the brightness of the picture. The deplorable habit is no where more lamentably conspicuous than at the Universities. It is truly sad to see these fine intelligent-looking young men, with the stupifying pipe continually in their hands, and the tobacco bag slung to their button-hole. Would it were possible to awaken their vanity to the effect which this nauseous practice produces on their appearance! At their age it would be so easy to break the habit! I really have sometimes almost wished, in pity, that the women smoked too. The contrast—the injustice, I may call it—is really too glaring. To expose these delicate, sweet-looking females to the real suffering, which the vicinity of breath infected by tobacco occasions, is positive cruelty.

How strange are the anomalies of the human mind! In the same country where the enthusiasm of sentiment is carried to the highest pitch, and cherished with the fondest reverence, the young men scruple not to approach the woman they love with sighs which make her turn her head aside, not to hide the blush of happiness, but the loathing of involuntary disgust.

But I have forgotten the Sunday evening at Godesberg; and must return to it, from the only circumstance which has left a disagreeable impression on my mind during my stay in Germany. I shall never forget the delight which four young students afforded us, after all the rattle of departing carriages was over, and a cool quiet evening had succeeded to a hot and bustling day. Seated at a little table near the door, they laid their pipes aside, and sang a quartet, of which the mere recollection gives a thrill of pleasure. What voices! what science! yet, this latter term can hardly, I think, be applied to them in the sense we generally use it when speaking of music: for we apply it only to those who have made harmony a long and elaborate study; and this can hardly be the case with these young men, or with the many others, whom we continually heard singing in parts, with such delicate perfection of time and tone, as we rarely find even in the most successful of our professors. "It comes by nature" to a German, and is certainly not the least among the many agreeable reminiscences which a sojourn among them enables one to lay up.

Before leaving Godesberg, we made an excursion to Bonn, by the river. This is a little voyage that should by no means be omitted. I doubt if any point of the Rhine, even between Coblentz and Mayence, offers scenery more lovely than that of the lake effects, produced by the turn of the river, which opens the view of the seven hills on one side, and the beautiful ruin of Godesberg Castle on the other.

My son found time, also, for a long ramble to the Eifel mountains; in the course of which he met with a very agreeable adventure. While inquiring his way to some point he was desirous to reach, he was addressed by a gentleman who resided in the neighbourhood; and after a short conversation accepted an invitation to his house.

This gentleman, an officer in the Prussian Lancers, is now on half-pay; and married to a very charming Englishwoman. Nothing could exceed the kindness and hospitality with which Henry was received into their house: and in addition to this, Captain —— had the kindness to accompany him to the Laacher See, a large and very remarkable lake in the neighbourhood. As this singular spot is quite out of the beat of most of our tourists, I will transcribe the account of it which I find in my son's journal; and also of the walk leading to it from the Rhine, as a guide to any who may have the will and power to visit it. The place at which he and his kind companion commenced their walk, was Unkel, a beautiful village on the eastern bank of the Rhine; and though this be a more distant point than any Rhenish traveller need start from, whose only object is to visit the Laacher See, I will give the whole of the long day's excursion, as it passes through a very interesting district.

"Leaving Unkel, we proceeded along the eastern bank of the Rhine; after an hour's walk we reached Erpel, an extensive village of poor *vignerons;* and a little beyond this is the celebrated basalt rock, called the Erpel Sei. It is of the columnar basalt; and is reckoned a very fine specimen; and so it certainly is in respect to its size; but, for the beauty of the columns, I prefer the quarries opposite Unkel, or Roland Seck; where there is a fine collection of bare columns heaped together in confused masses. From Erpel we continued our walk through the old city of Lintz, and under the interesting chateau of Argentfels, and passed through several small hamlets whose names have escaped me. Having reached Rheinbröhl, we crossed the Rhine, and entered the beautiful valley of the Brohl-thal, which runs nearly at right angles to the Rhine, and leads towards the Eifel mountains. We wound along this deep and narrow valley, till we reached the mineral spring of Toenstein, which, I believe, is a contraction for Antoenstein or Anthony's stone. The spring contains much fixed air, and tastes very much like soda water. We went into a little inn near the spring; and mixing wine and sugar with some of the water, it effervesced strongly, and made a very refreshing draught. A great quantity of this water is exported, and near the source is a manufactory of stone bottles for the purpose. Here we began to mount the steep hills to the left of the valley. My companion was highly agreeable and entertaining; and when the interest of the surrounding objects flagged, beguiled the way with amusing anecdotes of his military life, and by giving me much valuable information respecting the country. He spoke very highly of the Prussian system of making every man in the kingdom, of whatever rank, bear arms for three years. Even the king's sons are not exempt from this universal law: they wear the uniform, and do the duty of common soldiers, and stand guard before the palace of Berlin, with a musket on the shoulder. When in society, they wear the same dress as to form and colour; but are then permitted to have it made of a finer material. Captain —— told me that he had had the sons of princes in his troop; who did all the duty as privates, cleaned their own horses and arms, and stood the usual time on guard.

"As we mounted the hill, we began to see large masses of lava lying in all directions; and the crosses and crucifixes which stood thick upon the road-side are all carved from the same material. The soil here is not very good; and the farms are small and poor. Another hour's walking, the road rising steeply before us the whole way, brought us to Wapanach, a village not far from the lake we had come to see. Here we ordered our dinner at an inn, which was formerly the castle of a knight, who is said to have committed many black and fearful crimes, and afterwards to have taken refuge in the beautiful monastery, which is still to be seen in admirable preservation on the south-western corner of the lake—and there, *dit-on,* he ended his days.

"Leaving Wapanach behind us, we again toiled up to a great height through woods and corn-fields. The woods which surround the Laacher See are royal forest lands, and are of very great extent: they contain much game; deer and wild boars are very abundant in them. When we reached the skirts of this forest, we turned round, and resting on our staffs, enjoyed the magnificent view which this elevated spot commanded. In the distance was the high chain of the Westerwald, to which we looked across the charming valley of the Rhine. To the north were the towering tops of the Seven Mountains, with the singular basalt-capped hills of the Hochwald, speaking plainly of their violent and igneous birth; behind us were the Eifel mountains, on a small branch of which we stood; at our feet wound a little valley, deep sunk between the richly wooded and precipitous hills we had ascended.

"Having gazed on this landscape for a few minutes, we entered the wood; and descending for a short distance, came upon the Laacher See. It would be impossible for me to describe the astonishment I felt, even though prepared for the scene that opened upon me. I had just climbed to a great height, and but for a few moments before had been gazing upon distant valleys far beneath me, yet here I stood beside the blue expanse of an inland sea. It appeared to be the effect of magic, and I felt utterly confounded.

"The lake is a mile and half long, and a mile wide; it is surrounded on all sides by hills, without any visible outlet. To the north and east these hilly banks are very steep, and beautifully wooded to the water's edge, and the pendent boughs dip themselves in the lake. To the west the bank rises more gradually, and pastures border the water, reaching upward to the noble forest, which here also crowns the summit with a most luxuriant growth. To the south are bare, uncultivated peaks, which proclaim a volcanic origin; and their steril nakedness contrasts finely with the rich foliage and smiling meadows which surround the lake on the other sides. Vast masses of lava lie scattered round; and I have no doubt that they are right, who in this mountain lake think they discover the crater of an extinct volcano.

"The accounts given respecting its waters differ: while some assert that neither the heaviest rains nor the longest droughts ever cause them to rise or fall an inch; others relate, that the inhabitants of the monastery on its edge were once nearly overwhelmed by their sudden swell. This lake is of great depth,—some say it has never been fathomed; and the peasants all declare that bottom it has none. The waters are quite clear, and as blue as in the middle of the Atlantic."

Chapter VIII.

Rolandseck—Orlando Furioso—Nonnenwert — Unkel — Neuwied — Coblentz—The Moselle—Steam-boat Passengers—Mayence.

We were not sorry to hear that the delightful party at our table-d'hôte was to be broken up by the departure of some of its chief ornaments, on the same day that we had determined upon leaving Godesberg. Had it been otherwise, I think we should have looked behind us with too much regret to have permitted our fully enjoying the journeying forward. As it was, we said adieu as well as we might; and set off on the 17th July in *Mademoiselle's* rattling sociable for Rolandseck. This is a little hamlet of a few houses only, situated at the foot of a basaltic rock, on the summit of which stands the lonely tower of Roland.

Having been assured that this scathed and crumbling fragment was built by no less a wight than the luckless, but magnificent hero of Ariosto, I could not resist my inclination to halt beneath it.

The situation, indeed, is attractive enough to justify the loitering of a day, even to those who felt no interest in the ruin. Exactly opposite to Rolandseck is the pretty island of Nonnenwert, on which stands a very noble mansion, formerly a nunnery, but now a most delightful hotel. Here we decided upon passing the night; after devoting an hour or two to climbing the hill, examining the wonderful formation of basalt of which it is composed, and peering into every nook and cranny of Orlando's Castle. It cannot be denied, I fear, that this idol of romancers was a very faithless and fickle lover; and, questionless, the departure of his wits to the moon was a punishment for his infidelities.

It was one of his numerous love affairs which led to the construction of this most desolate dwelling-place upon the rock above Rolandseck. Its legend tells of a noble maiden, who, having won the love of the hot-brained Paladin, preferred the sheltering cloister of Nonnenwert to all the worldly pleasures he could offer. Whereupon he built this lonely tower, that he might look upon the roof which sheltered her. But even this sad consolation was not long enjoyed, for one evening, as he stood before his tower, he saw the whole train of nuns issue from the principal gate of the building, and wind round to the entrance of the vaults beneath the chapel. Here they stopped; and a coffin was borne forward from among them, under the low arch of the tomb. The plaintive notes of a funeral chant reached his ear,—his heart told him it was the requiem for his love. Darting from the place where he stood, he dashed down the face of the precipice, springing from rock to rock till he reached the bottom; on arriving there he mounted his war-horse, which ever stood ready, and galloped off to King Charlemagne's court at Aix.

Those who recall this tale while the Rolandseck rock rises before their eyes, will allow it to be in keeping with many of the feats recorded by Ariosto of this same fiery hero.

As we mounted the zigzag terraces of the vine-covered hill, on which the ruin stands, the notes of a duet of Mozart's, most deliciously sung, reached us by snatches from two young men, who came bounding down the declivity towards us. They politely stood aside, and ceased their song as we passed. I would rather have been rudely jostled had they but continued it. But we stopped to listen, after they had passed the next turning; and again we heard their rich young voices, like the music of Ariel, floating about us.

It is difficult to give an idea of the sort of magical effect produced by hearing sounds so sweet, and so perfect in their artist-like harmony, from among trees and rocks and desert wildernesses. Often as this happened during our journey, I never ceased to experience from it all the delight produced by pleasure when completely unexpected.

Having been told to see the sun set from Roland's tower, we contrived that so it should be ; and I beg to transmit the same recommendation to all who may chance to follow in our track. It must have been from some such spot, and at such an hour, that Claude studied those effects of light and darkness which " enchant the world."

On descending from Rolandseck, we crossed to the island of Nonnenwert, with just light enough left to show us the most perfect reflections on the water that I ever saw.

As it is my especial ambition that these volumes should become a profitable guide-book to all who may travel by the route they describe, I will venture, even at the risk of being tedious, to dwell a little upon the charms of this beautiful island, and on the peculiar interest of its solitary mansion. I am principally led to do so by the statement of our host at the hotel; who told me that before steam-boats were established on the Rhine, all travellers, especially the English, used to come in crowds to his house, and pass a week or fortnight there, exploring the country on both sides, in every direction: "But now," he added piteously, " they drive past, as fast as they can go, and never set foot on shore, except at night, from Rotterdam to Mayence."

Though not so deeply interested in the affair as the innkeeper, I really lament this alteration in the mode of travelling; for I am convinced that the expressions of disappointment, which we must all have occasionally heard of late from our touring friends, respecting the scenery of this celebrated river, arise chiefly from the earlier pictures of it having been given by such as have loitered through every "dingle and bushy dell" upon its banks. Those who have watched its majestic waters, not from the crowded stern of a steamboat, but while luxuriating in the shelter of some deep cool valley, winding upward from its banks; or have looked down upon them from the dark shade of a ruined watch-tower, perched so high as to make the broad stream itself but a small feature in the landscape; or indulged themselves, perhaps, for hours in gazing when, lovelier still, its bosom gave back the bright image of a moon-lit sky, while rocks and ruins hung their black shadows over it, —may well paint it differently from the tourist of later days; who knows it only by standing on the deck of a vessel, with a panoramic view of the Rhine in his hand, turning his head this side to see one ruin, and that side to see another :—his finger placed with nervous eagerness upon some famous promontory, and his thumb on a first-rate castle,—while kept in a state of feverish agitation lest the panting engine should bear him out of reach before he can get a peep at either.

Before this mode of seeing the Rhine became the fashion, Nonnenwert was one of the favourite points at which travellers took up their rest; and there are a multitude of reasons, both real and fanciful, that render it a spot of peculiar attraction. The real reasons must of course rank first; and these are,—its possessing the very best accommodation in every way; excellent rooms, excellent cuisine, excellent wines; and though last not least, its being in a neighbourhood abounding with objects of every kind that can most interest an intelligent traveller. For its fanciful advantages—it might perhaps be wiser to keep them to myself; and so I would, did I not believe that many others would feel as much gratification as I did, in exploring every part of this magnificent nunnery, with all its distinctive features carefully preserved, and the traces of its late holy tenants still legible on every part of it.

Nonnenwert was a very rich establishment for

a numerous society of noble recluses, when Napoleon took possession of the country. He signified his will that it should share the fate of all the similar institutions which had fallen into his hands. But, by some means or other, the holy ladies got access to Josephine; and received her promise, that she would use all her influence to obtain permission from the Emperor for them to keep possession of their island and their fane, as long as any of them should survive. This was granted, but on express condition that no new sisters were to be received. For several years the society continued to exist, though gradually decreasing. Nothing, as my informant told me, and she knew them well, could be more mournful than the meeting of this lessening band at the hours of re-union. The stately gallery of the chapel, which formerly was hardly large enough to hold them, seemed, as the melancholy remnant entered it, to stretch over the tombs below, only to show the graves that waited for them.

While the abbess lived, the remaining sisters dreamed not of the possibility of leaving her: but when they lost her, the survivors, then reduced to six, had not courage to watch further the work of death within their little circle; each perhaps hoping, yet fearing, to be the last. It was too much even for the disciplined spirits of nuns to bear: so they disposed of their remaining interest in the island, and each retired to such relations and friends as their long seclusion had left them.

I heard this history from one who had resided in the convent during its last sad years; and though neither old nor ugly, it was evident that she did not consider the destruction of a convent as a jubilee for its inmates.

It has been probably with a view of increasing the attractions of his establishment to foreigners, that the present proprietor of Nonnenwert has suffered the monastery to remain so nearly in the same state as when inhabited by its nuns. The building is very extensive, and in many respects extremely handsome. Several noble flights of stairs lead from the chambers below to a magnificent corridor, which runs round the whole edifice; and though its vast extent receives no light except from the large high windows at each corner, it is rather solemn than dark. A row of low doors, very low in proportion to the great height of the galleries, open on either side; and mark the cells, which, at no very distant period, were the abode of some of the noblest ladies in Germany. Many of these remain exactly as they were, and make very comfortable sleeping-rooms; those on one side looking into a large quadrangle, surrounded by the venerable cloister, and now laid out as a flower-garden; and those on the other commanding some of the finest views on the Rhine.

As we were led through this echoing gallery to the apartments destined for us, we passed before a door, which, instead of being low like the others, was lofty and folding. It stood partly open, and the attendant, who preceded us, pushed it together, but not so as completely to close it. Being a few steps behind my companions, and feeling curious to know to what this stately doorway could lead, I put my hand upon the heavy lock, pulled it open and entered; when I was startled to find myself in a wide gallery, which overhung the chapel. It was very nearly dark; and the little light left just served to make every object look like something it was not. Monumental figures had the air of kneeling nuns; and the very altars seemed full of shapeless mystery. I quickly retreated and overtook my companions, who were pausing before another lofty door, which, on being opened, discovered an interior staircase; and beyond it still, another high and handsome folding door, leading into a very noble saloon. This chamber, and another still grander room, that was shown us next day, were formerly used on state occasions, when the Elector of Cologne held a court at Nonnenwert.

Having signified our approbation of this apartment, the attendant led the way to a *ci-devant* cell beside it; and asked, if that sleeping chamber would please Madame? Nothing could be more comfortable than its appearance. The window looked upon Rolandseck, now visible by the moonlight; and after admiring this for a moment, I turned to examine another window, over which a curtain was drawn. On removing it, I perceived that the casement it covered was open; and that I again looked down upon the gloomy chapel. As I do not profess a belief in supernatural visitations, I am rather at a loss to account for the sudden distaste I conceived for this pretty little cell as a sleeping apartment. Certain it is, however, that I chose another.

When going over the house on the following morning, I asked my conductor to show me the late abbess's room: but this, she said, she could not do, as it was occupied by an English clergyman, who had been some weeks in the house, together with two or three young men, whom she believed to be his pupils. She added, that he read English prayers in the gallery of the chapel; and that one or two English families in the neighbourhood joined his little congregation every Sunday. I could not learn his name from her, though she tried to recall it; which I regretted, as I should have been happy to have learned who the gentleman was who showed so excellent a taste in his choice of a retreat for the purposes of study.

Before leaving the island, we carefully explored

every part of it. The undertaking was not one of much fatigue: for the extent of this pretty territory does not exceed one hundred and sixty acres; but the views from the different parts of it are very beautiful. To the north is the "castled crag of Drachenfels," infinitely finer when seen from thence than in any other direction. To the east is the opening of the wavy valley of the Rhine; on one of whose sunny slopes a brother of Lord Portarlington has made for himself a little paradise. To the west stands the melancholy, but most picturesque tower of Rolandseck, with the octagon columns of its basaltic rock; and to the south the Rhine loses itself among mountains that shut it in like a lake.

The chief part of the island is occupied by a large wheat-field; but near the house are ample gardens and orchards: and the whole extent of its shores have a growth of underwood, affording innumerable pretty nooks for the sketchers or gazers who wish to study, in shade and at ease, the lovely scenes that present themselves in all directions.

At eleven o'clock we took a reluctant leave of

this sweet and quiet spot; and having hired a little skiff for the purpose, were towed up the river to Unkel. I had here the pleasure of being introduced to my son's agreeable new friends, and found them all he had described. There are some incidents in life that make a deep impression, more from the manner in which they occur than from their real importance. Such, perhaps, was the case as to my short but delightful visit at Unkel. The frank, gentlemanly cordiality of Captain ———; the bright, glowing animation of his charming dark-eyed wife, as she welcomed a countrywoman; their lovely children; their elegant yet perfectly rustic dwelling, with its books and its music, its flowers and its vines,—had altogether something so very delightful to the heart and the fancy, that, after it was all over, and we had got on board the steam-boat for Coblentz—after we had seen them wave their last adieu from the shore, and finally lost sight of Unkel and of them—I could hardly persuade myself that the last hour had not been passed in a delightful dream.

The waking, however, was not so painful as one

sometimes feels it, when obliged to give up all the bright nothings of a morning vision: for a sober and certain recollection remained of having met a group of just such beings as one should like to see the world peopled withal. Nothing tends more to put one in good humour with oneself and everything else than such an adventure; and I am certain that the *bergs* and the *steins*, the *fels* and the *thals*, by which we flew along on our way to Coblentz, appeared vastly more beautiful than they would have done without it. Nevertheless, the river is " an exulting and abounding river;" and dash through it as rapidly as you may, it has beauty which will make itself felt.

The appearance of the flourishing town of Neuwied is striking, from its great dissimilarity to all others on the Rhine. It is not a hundred years since it was founded, 1737 being the date of its oldest edifice. It has been the pleasure, or the policy of its prince, not only to tolerate, but to encourage the residence of every denomination of religionists; and the consequence is that the population of Neuwied more resembles that of an

American than of a German town. Its present prince has a very pretty chateau and park on the hills which inclose the vast amphitheatre in which the town is situated. To this he has given the name of " Mon Repos ; " but it is rarely, it seems, that he permits himself to enjoy it. He is a great naturalist; and his love of science has led him rather to an enterprising than a luxurious existence. He is now residing, we were told, for the second time, among the native tribes of South America.

The approach to Coblentz is very grand. The commanding fortress of Ehrenbreitstein, showing no longer a " shattered wall," but magnificent in its extent of splendid masonry, spreads far and wide over the rock that fronts the city, on the opposite side of the river. The Moselle and the Rhine unite at the point at which the city of Coblentz is built; and all the elevated points on the banks of either are covered with fortifications.

As soon as we had secured apartments, we set off to wander through the town; and to see as much of the Moselle as a walk of two hours would show us. On our way we passed the monument erected in the market-place; which has perhaps caused as much strong feeling as any that ever was constructed. The inscription is as follows:—

Anno 1812.
Mémorable par la Campagne contre les Russes, sous le Préfecture de Jules Douzan.

Vu, et approuvé par nous, Commandant Russe de la Ville de Coblentz, le 1ʳᵉ Janvier, 1814.

This presumptuous and ill-advised monument was erected by Napoleon, when on his route to Russia; and the biting addition to the inscription was subjoined, after his discomfiture, in a spirit easily understood, and easily to be justified. Yet I almost started as I read it; and thought the wit something in the style of the jokes indulged in by Petit André, when hanging up his merry playfellows on the gallows-tree. I should have liked it better had I heard of it as uttered at a mess-table, than seeing it as thus inscribed on brass.

We crossed the bridge over the Moselle, which is here certainly less "blue" than brown; but ere we returned from our excursion, we saw it enter a defile of wooded hills, which made us long to follow it.

The bridge itself, as well as every avenue leading to it, appear to be as powerfully protected by fortifications as the art of the engineer can make them; and there is no part of the city more picturesque and interesting. The buildings, particularly the more ancient ones, are of that strange incomprehensible shape which sets the imagination at work to discover what such mysterious turrets could be intended for; and why such depth and height of walls should ever have been fabricated without a window. It is very certain, that if there be infinite delight in seeing and understanding clearly on some occasions, there is almost equal pleasure, at others, in losing oneself in wild conjecture; and permitting the mind to wander as far as possible from well-established facts, and the sober certainty of every-day life.

Yet, with all this, I did not greatly admire the appearance of the city. But this might be owing solely to my finding no fine churches in it. To a peaceable Christian, like myself, the sight of a magnificent fortress is certainly less attractive than that of a magnificent cathedral.

The next morning, at five o'clock, we were again afloat; and had not left Coblentz many hours before it was decided among us, that such a country as we were then passing must not be so looked at for the last time. A short consultation of the map, joined to the flying glances we were able to take of all that was flitting by, soon decided how, when, and where we should fix ourselves for the purpose of seeing with pleasure the objects which it almost put us out of breath to enumerate as we shot past them. This resolution once taken, I relaxed in some degree from the labour of twisting my neck this way and that way to look at the banks; and ventured to give some portion of my attention to the scene on board. It must be confessed that there is something very amusing in the humours of a steam-boat, when one takes leisure to observe them. Our "Princess Marianne," however, had none of the vulgar features of a Margate packet. Nothing vulgar, in the ordinary sense of the word, met the eye in any direction; but there was a good deal of *genteel comedy*, which it was the more agreeable to watch, as all the actors in it appeared extremely happy.

My first study was a newly married pair. That they were such could not admit of a doubt. They were English, and came on board at Coblentz, with a handsome carriage, a smart man and maid servant, but no companion save each other. It was evident, that he wanted no other: she was very pretty, and he was decidedly very much in love. Had she possessed but two grains more intelligence, the little scenes that passed between them would have been sacred, rather than ridiculous: but who could resist a smile at seeing the frequent yawn, hid in the embroidered handkerchief, as the enamoured young man sought to raise some of the delightful sensations he felt himself, by reading in her ear from a beautiful pocket Byron? I doubt not but the lines—

"Could thy dear eyes in following mine
　Still sweeten more these banks of Rhine,"

were among his selections. But it would not do: her eyes did not follow—nay, they did not even meet his. He was so really amiable and animated in his endeavours to amuse this fair automaton, that I sat musing as to what could be passing in her mind to render her so completely callous to all he could say or do; and at last I unravelled the mystery. It was not that she had given her hand without her heart—it was not that her fancy wandered back to some one more beloved—it was simply—that she was hungry.

After a long silence on her part, she whispered something in his ear; he darted from her side, gave a look forward, as I fancied for his servant, but not seeing him, ran down the cabin-stairs himself with dangerous velocity, and after a short interval, returned with tidings which seemed greatly to cheer his companion. Again he sought to amuse her by reading—in vain. " To beguile the time," he should have " looked like the time," which was —of luncheon. At length a waiter appeared with a tray of smoking cutlets. I could hardly wonder that the young man was anxious to please his pretty bride; for I never saw smile more bright and beautiful than the one she gave him, as he prepared her plate, and arranged her feet upon a footstool, so as to make it steady on her lap. I only wished, for his sake, that it had been born of a more sentimental cause than the apparition of a mutton steak. Yet after all it was hardly fair to quiz her for it. She had probably breakfasted at a miserably early hour; and who, under such circumstances, but would have smiled as sweetly as they could?

Another group, forming perhaps a fairer subject for pleasantry, consisted of a handsome woman, but not quite young, and a magnificent *militaire*, not quite old. They were certainly not married, nor were they English. It was one of those vehement flirtations, which, if carried on at all, should find a less public scene of action than the deck of a steam-boat.

Close by these, but quite unheeded by them, stood a pair of young ladies, sketching in two little books, à l'envie l'une de l'autre. It seemed to be a match against time, as well as against each other; and the odds were a hundred to one against their finishing the first turret of their castle, before it was half a mile behind them.

Then there were bustling young men, of more nations thon one, twisting about, guide-book in hand, and occasionally enjoying the landscape through an eye-glass. Some of these I observed to be great linguists, who would probably have found little difficulty in pursuing their labours even in the tower of Babel. I heard one of them address a boatman on coming on board as follows:—" Woolen sie put cela avec the baggage?" But the man seemed used to the style, and testified neither surprise nor merriment.

The multitude of " chiefless castles," with which this part of the river is studded, is prodigious; and as old records speak not much of the peaceable temper of their former lords, the neighbourhood must, in days of yore, have been a rough one to dwell in. Every little town, too, by the water's side, is fenced about with towers and battlements; and tell sad tales of the rude visitings they expected to receive.

Travelling upon the Rhine is like reading a romance in hieroglyphics. Not a mile, often not half a one, is passed without coming upon some object, which, to the very dullest fancy, must suggest ideas of power, of pomp, of struggle and renown, of danger and of death. The very act of building these eagles' nests on pinnacles which few tame animals would venture to climb, speaks a sort of daring hardihood, somewhat difficult to be understood in these days of peaceful comfort. As to the lovely ladies, of whom chronicles say that every castle made its boast, they must have been drawn up by windlasses; for in no other way, I think, could they have ever reached some of the strong-holds which stand so grimly alone upon the mountain-tops.

Unfortunately, these interesting remains came thicker and faster upon us as the hour of dinner approached; and when we were actually seated at table, notice was given, by such as caught a passing glance through the windows, of such wondrous congregations of fortified towns, mouldering monasteries, and castled crags, that half the company started upon their feet, and the other half nearly choked themselves in the hope of getting their dinner despatched before all the ruins were out of sight. Had the ruthless spirits of the barons themselves animated these towers, over which they once held cruel sway, even they could hardly have desired to produce upon us, by their aspect, more distressing effects. The seats of one-half the company being fixed to the sides of the vessel, those who occupied them had to creep under the table every time a fresh burst of enthusiasm arose. This happened no less than three times, during the dinner of this day, to a French gentleman, who sat immediately opposite to me. Had I or my neighbours been ferociously disposed, it would have been easy to have "whipped the offending Adam out of him," for he grovelled in so extraordinary a manner among the feet of the company before he could extricate himself, that the visual organs he was so anxious to indulge ran great risk of being severely damaged, if not destroyed for ever.

Though I had previously decided upon indulging myself with another and more tranquil survey of the objects we were passing, I at last left the table in utter despair of being permitted to sit at it with any degree of comfort, and went upon deck, not so much for the sake of seeing what was indeed very beautiful, as to escape suffering from the fitful fever of my opposite neighbour, who ceased not to crawl forth when castles came; yet, whenever we passed a few yards without one, never failed to return, with renewed appetite, to his chicken bones and Moselle.

Those who choose to see the Rhine from a steam-boat, should decidedly make up their minds not to eat dinners between Cologne and Mayence; or, if this exceed their power, they should content themselves with eating, like my fair bride, with their plate upon their knees, without quitting the deck; and so placed as to enable them to look on either side with as little dislocation of the neck as possible.

It must not be thought, however, that because I sometimes withdrew my eyes from the landscape to look at my neighbours I was insensible to the great beauty, nay, sublimity, of the scenery between Coblentz and Mayence. This part of the river is by far the most beautiful; and there are some points which rather exceeded than fell short of the expectations I had formed.

While remarking the inconvenience which a too rapid mode of travelling through scenes so beautiful occasions, I remembered that nearly all I had seen of the Hudson was while running up and down it in a steam-boat:—and, though the movement was at least as rapid, or even more so, I could not recall anything like the same vexation from the circumstance. The reason of this, certainly, is not that the Hudson is less beautiful;— on the contrary, I think the scenery near West Point, and, generally speaking, the whole of that portion called the Highlands, decidedly superior to any part of the Rhine:—but it arises from the infinite variety of interest which the combinations of history and romance throw over every inch of the European stream.

I well remember that I thought we passed too quickly by the tree under which poor André was made prisoner; and that I gazed upon the spot till I could see it no longer. But when this was over, the banks of the Hudson had nothing but their own loveliness to fill the mind; and though this be much, the spirit enjoys it more tranquilly than when a thousand associations rouse up as many different springs of feeling in the heart.

Before reaching Mayence the banks of the river become comparatively tame; soon after Bingen the rocks cease altogether; and hanging slopes, covered with vineyards, take their place. The far-famed hill of Johannisberg, with the mansion of Prince Metternich on its summit, is seen rising in terraces from the plain which skirts the water's edge, rich in its precious growth of unequalled wine.

The almost unvaried continuance of the vineyards is certainly a great defect in the scenery of the Rhine; but here again association helps to make us regard with pleasure what is neither beautiful nor sublime. For who can look upon the promise of so much wealth and enjoyment, and wish it other than it is? The delicious Stein wine is cause of least offence in this respect; for the grape from which it is made grows almost from the fissures of the rocks, and in little patches of such wild irregularity, as rather to increase than diminish the charm of the prospect.

Bieberich, the magnificent palace of the Duke of Nassau, is a splendid ornament to the scenery on the eastern bank, a few miles below Mayence; and the fortresses of Castel and Kostheim, with the bridge of boats, and the picturesque towers of the cathedral, all contribute to make the approach to the city, by water, a scene of great beauty and interest.

Chapter IX.

Mayence—Cathedral—Francfort—Theatre—Cathedral —St. Catherine's — Cemetery—Jewish Synagogue— Luther—Hesse-Homberg.

MAYENCE is another very interesting old city, as I think everybody must allow; but I believe the report of its claims to beauty will depend greatly upon the temper of the traveller, according to the principle laid down in Franklin's story of the man with one handsome and one ugly leg. The good-tempered traveller will remember its handsomest streets and public buildings, its beautiful gardens, and the picturesque effect of its multitude of Asiatic-looking domes and minarets; but the cross or melancholy traveller will not easily forget its narrower streets, its dirty pavement, or its villanous smells. Its beautiful situation, however, none can fail to acknowledge; and it has the great advantage of being situated within easy reach of many places of first-rate attraction. Francfort, Wiesbaden, Ingleheim, and all the beauties of the lovely Rhingau, are within a morning's ride of Mayence.

This city is one of those which severally claim the glory of having witnessed the invention of printing within their walls; and it stoutly vindicates its pretension, in spite of all that Strasburg or Haarlem can adduce to the contrary. The house where Gutenberg first used his moveable types is shown as one of the proudest boasts of the city.

The cathedral is large and splendid, but by no means beautiful. It has, in fact, been so battered and bruised by the eternal wars of which Mayence has been the victim, that it is now little more than a vast and costly mass of reparations. The monuments, which have been wonderfully preserved, are highly curious:—that of Fastrada, one of the wives of Charlemagne, bearing date 794, and another of the old troubadour Frauenlob, 1218, cannot be seen with indifference.

Archbishops and Electors lie here in great magnificence. Among the latter are some who assisted at the coronation of more than one Emperor;—a piece of good fortune quaintly commemorated on their tombs. There is one monument of great antiquity, on which the effigies of the entombed Elector is represented as putting crowns on the brows of two imperial personages, whose figures kneeling before him seem to knock their heads together in order to place them conveniently for receiving the symbols of empire.

There are two high altars in this church; one at the east, the other at the west end: the same thing, I am told, is to be seen at Spires and at Worms, but no where else. The effect is very strange. The font of bronze, of the year 1325, is superb; and the brass doors, which open from the market-place, and which are of a still earlier date, are wonderfully ingenious and elaborate.

But the object which pleased me most, in this strange collection of old and new curiosities, was a fine antique head of Jupiter, in white marble. It is placed beneath a monument fixed in the wall, at the north-east corner of the church, near the door which leads out to the cloisters; but how it came there we could by no means learn. The head is set between wings; the finish of these, the graceful flow of the beard, with the noble expression of the imperial countenance, are all admirable.

Mayence is garrisoned by Prussians and Austrians;—I believe, in equal numbers. It is considered as one of the most important fortresses of the Germanic Confederation. The civil department belongs to the duchy of Hesse Darmstadt; and a few soldiers of that state are seen mixed among the Austrians and Prussians, who do the military duties of the garrison.

On the following day we started for Francfort by the diligence, and were nearly four hours on the road. We passed by the little village of Hockheim, and looked with great respect towards the vineyards which we were told produced the genuine Hockheimer.

On our way we saw a village funeral, and it appeared as though the whole of the rustic population had left their labour, to do honour to the dead: for above two hundred peasants followed the corpse. The females walked first, all dressed in decent black gowns and white hoods; the men following in their ordinary Sunday attire.

Almost as soon as you enter Francfort, you become aware of its neatness, its beauty, its venerable antiquity, and its modern splendour. Francfort has no "ugly leg" to remark upon, and the most splenetic traveller must, I think, allow himself to be pleased by the numerous *agrémens* it has to offer.

We fixed ourselves in the *Hôtel de Paris*, where we found excellent accommodation: and, after a breakfast *à la fourchette*, set forth to perambulate the town. However impatient we felt to see the streets and examine the buildings, it was quite impossible to resist the trees and flowers which drew us aside, ere we had proceeded a hundred yards, into the beautiful public garden that entirely surrounds the city. The beauty, salubrity, and luxury of this arrangement, cannot be fully appreciated without visiting this delightful place. I never saw such a profusion of flowers, and flowering shrubs, in any other garden; and the manner in which the walks are planned, sometimes running through narrow and shady alleys, and sometimes opening into broad and handsome promenades, leaves nothing to be wished for.

It was not without difficulty that I was at last persuaded to turn from this beautiful garden towards the streets of the town;—nor did I leave it till I had walked for nearly a mile through roses, carnations, lilies, honeysuckles, and everything else of the sweetest and best which a garden can present.

Why is it impossible to teach my dear countrymen and countrywomen that flowers may be enjoyed without the assistance of the fingers? Had the gardens of Francfort been inclosed by a wall as high as that of Babylon, the preservation of the flowers could not have been more perfect:—yet groups of children were playing in every direction, and the benches were occupied by people of all degrees. It must, however, be confessed, that at Francfort, this expression includes nothing either disorderly or sordid—at least I saw no such persons.

Having at length re-entered the town, we wandered on through handsome streets and noble squares, till I was too tired to do more than return, by the shortest cut we could find, to our hotel.

We had previously decided upon passing our evening at the theatre, and found it necessary to hurry through our dinner, as the performance was to begin at six. Mrs. K., the lady of the British consul, had obligingly offered us places in her box.

The first impression on entering the Francfort theatre is made by the extreme plainness of the house. I never saw any so little ornamented, and it can hardly be doubted that a little more decoration would be an improvement.

The play was "The Brothers,"—a very close translation of "The Woman never Vexed." The acting was excellent; and, spite of our imperfect German, we had no difficulty in following the fable throughout.

Though, I fear, it would be impossible for us, or, perhaps, any other people than Germans, to follow the example, I must still say a few words upon some peculiarities of the Francfort theatre; as it is, in my judgment, more completely what a place of this kind ought to be, than any I ever saw or heard of. The absence of ornament in the part occupied by the audience, is its only defect, and is, perhaps, of no great importance: nay, it probably adds to the splendid effect of the scene. But the first indisputable excellence I shall mention, is its size. A more just medium could hardly be imagined, between the vastness which obliges the performer to distort, if I may so express it, bot features and voice, and the diminutiveness, which would not permit even full houses to furnish funds sufficient to supply the expenses of a first-rate performance. Its next advantage consists in giving one piece only:—the entertainment continues just long enough to amuse without fatiguing. But the last, and infinitely the greatest excellence, consists in the manners of the audience, in which there is such an entire absence of every species of indecorum, as to render the theatre as safe as the drawing-room. The consequence is, that females of all ranks enter it, with as much modest, unembarrassed freedom, as they would their homes; and they are equally secure there from insult or alarm as they would be at home.

Nearly all the boxes are let by the year; and the ladies enter them alone, without fuss or parade of any kind. I saw several ladies (who, as I happened to know, had come there in their carriages) take off their bonnets, and hang them on the pins with which the back of every box is furnished, with a degree of unembarrassed ease and comfort which was quite delightful.

The evening parties take place after the play or opera: and as the dinner-hour is generally early, the performances interfere with nothing. In a word, the theatre of Francfort is so arranged, as to add a great intellectual pleasure to life, without any one drawback whatsoever.

The following day was Sunday. We first attended mass in the Catholic cathedral, and the Lutheran service afterwards in the new oval church of St. Paul's. In the afternoon we heard another Lutheran service performed at St. Catherine's. The Catholic cathedral is said to be the latest specimen of genuine old German architecture; it was completed in 1509; and is built in the form of a cross. It has little beauty of any kind to recommend it; but as it has been neither injured nor embellished by any alterations, it forms an interesting specimen. The machinery of a huge clock, curious from the extreme complexity of its movements, is shown among other " lions" of the edifice. No stately monuments of Archbishops and Electors are to be seen here, but there are tombs of Burgomasters innumerable. There are, moreover, some Knights Templars buried in this cathedral, whose martial trophies adorn the walls with very picturesque effect. The chancel, which is very large, was most completely crowded in every part. One priest alone officiated at the altar, and he had not the tonsure:—we counted thirteen at the celebration of high mass at Cologne. This difference is very remarkable, and would seem to indicate that the wealth, which flows so liberally into Francfort, does not find its way into the hands of the Catholics. The congregation consisted evidently of the lower classes; and the crowd which filled the aisles so closely, as to render it impossible to pass through them, had chiefly the air of peasants of the neighbourhood. The female head-dress among them was extremely neat and pretty; particularly for matrons. It consisted of a small silk cap, generally black, with a ribbon bound over the neatly braided hair, and hanging in long bows and streamers behind. But I thought it less becoming to the young; as it concealed too much of the luxuriant hair, which is so beautiful a feature in German girls.

The new Lutheran church is a magnificent temple. It is an immense oval, with a vaulted roof of great height and boldness. Three light and elegant galleries run round the lofty walls. The lowest of these is supported by twenty noble pillars of marble. This church, also, was completely full, and offered a most brilliant *coup-d'œil*; the ladies filling the entire floor, and the gentlemen the galleries, or the space immediately under them. Of the multitude who filled this vast church, there was not a single individual who was not perfectly well-dressed. It was decidedly the most elegant-looking assembly I ever saw in a church. That at the Catholic cathedral at Baltimore approached the nearest to it; but the company there was neither so numerous nor so well displayed. This beautiful edifice was just completed ; and I thought it a piece of good fortune not to have arrived till it was so.

The old church of St. Catherine's, founded by a Knight Templar, is well worth visiting. It is now Lutheran; and we there heard one of those glorious universal hymns, which when they rise from a congregation of German voices, produce an effect so indescribably solemn and affecting, as never to be forgotten.

This reformed old church looks as if it had resigned the ancient faith reluctantly, at least as to outward appearance; for the symbols of Catholicism are still visible in every part of it. Pictures, crosses and carved representations of the Passion abound. The only conspicuous change is at the altar, from which the ark for the elements of the Eucharist, and the great candlesticks, have been removed, and the whole covered with plain velvet. It has a fine altar-piece by Boos. The walls of this church are literally covered from top to bottom with monuments.

In the evening we went to the Opera, and were again kindly admitted to Mrs. K———'s box. The performance was the Vestalin of Spontini. It is a delightful opera, and was most gloriously performed. The choruses have an effect, at least when performed by Germans, which I am at a loss how to describe:—they are sounds of feeling, of passion, and of eloquence. The indignation I have experienced from seeing the plays of Shakspeare turned into operas, would have been spared, I think, had I heard them performed here. Never was music so lawfully " married to immortal verse" as in this country.

Mademoiselle Gned, who played the part of Julia, has a voice of great power; but as yet it seems almost more than she can manage. She has great merit also as an actress, and showed much animation and feeling;—but she should study the perfect harmony of Pasta's movements. It is no trifling addition to the pleasure of an opera where we can say of the prima donna—

" Where'er she turns, the Graces homage pay;"
and, as a lady's raised arms must either "float upon

the air," or pierce through it, it is well worth some study to acquire the power of choosing which it shall be. Mademoiselle Gned is, however, a young actress of great promise, and two or three years will probably bring her into general notice.

How delightful it is to come away from such an entertainment as this with the spirits perfectly fresh and unwearied! Instead of dragging to bed, with the head aching, the heart asleep, and the imagination utterly extinguished, we leave the theatres of Germany exactly in a state to feel, or fancy ourselves above all mortal cares and discomforts; and, I think, the evening parties which succeed them must see the very best of our social faculties in activity.

I had the pleasure, on this evening, of being introduced to Madame Goethe, the daughter-in-law of the immortal poet and philosopher. She is a lady of very pleasing manners, and has an air of great intelligence and animation; she speaks English of the most perfect purity and elegance. It seemed to me no small privilege to hold converse with a person bearing a name so illustrious.

After the opera we went to the public gardens near the river; we were told that they had been extremely full, but the company were then departing rapidly. The orchestra, chiefly of wind instruments, performed some pieces of Mozart very beautifully; but, as about two men out of every three we met (let the companion beside each be as lovely as she might) were armed with that instrument of torture a tobacco-pipe, these gardens, when most brilliantly filled, could not be agreeable to me. Happily, smoking is not allowed in theatres or drawing-rooms; and as long as this continues to be the case, it is very possible, by a little skill and good management, to confine one's sufferings from this source to the sorrow arising from the sight of so glaring a defect, in a people so admirable in other respects.

I was surprised at being told, in answer to an inquiry on the subject, which I addressed to a Protestant, that the Calvinists and Lutherans frequent the Sunday opera, quite as much as any other people. The only difference, indeed, which I perceived at Francfort, from towns entirely Catholic, was, that no shops were open on a Sunday; and this I was assured arose from no religious restraint, but solely from such a degree of ease in the general circumstances of the citizens, as rendered attention to business on the seventh day quite unnecessary. The same reason causes all the shops in the town to be closed at seven o'clock every evening, as no one will suffer business to interfere with his hours of recreation.

There certainly is, however, something very remarkable in the religious aspect of Francfort. I believe there is no denomination of Christians, which cannot be found there; each of them having one or more places of worship. These are uniformly filled twice every Sunday with devout and observant congregations. But, at about six o'clock, every church and chapel is closed; and, from that hour, there is scarcely an individual to be found who is not actively engaged in the pursuit of pleasure. Catholic and Protestant, Calvinist and Lutheran, all join in the universal jubilee. The wide circuit of the public walks is gaily filled in every part; the theatre overflows; the cafés and guinguettes are thronged; and I was assured that dancing, music, and feasting, are universally, and equally, enjoyed by all sects and denominations throughout the city.

It should seem from this, that the lawgivers of this *Freistadt* act much upon the same principles as did our first King Charles, of pious memory, and his martyred Protestant Archbishop Laud, when they put forth "The Book of Sports;" which not only legalized, but enjoined, diversions for the people on the Sunday.

Another circumstance, which is remarkable, when viewed together with this manner of passing the Christian sabbath, is, that on Friday evenings, after the Jewish sabbath has begun, the theatre is always closed. Why this is thought necessary no one could tell me;—though all allowed that it was done "because it was the Jews' sabbath." At the same hour on Saturday, when this rigid Jewish observance ends, Jews and Christians are again permitted to amuse themselves. The proportion of Jews to Protestant Christians is stated to be about one to ten.

Whether anything like poverty, or real want, is to be found at Francfort, I know not; but certainly nothing approaching it ever meets the eye; nor did I ever see any place so perfectly well ordered, and free from nuisances of all kinds.

I had a great deal of conversation on the politics of this fair and free city, with a gentleman who has long resided there. He told me, that no people could be better satisfied with the laws that governed them, than the citizens of Francfort; and stated, as a proof of it, their having witnessed, with so much approbation, the arrival of Prussian and Austrian troops, when some political disturbances appeared to threaten the stability of their institutions. He spoke with great indignation of the injustice of foreign newspapers, and particularly of the English, for representing the riotous frolic of a few noisy young men, as affording indications of a general revolutionary spirit.

I will transcribe his words as I find them in my notes, having set them down immediately after the conversation took place.

"C'était une bonne plaisanterie de voir courir de journal en journal l'effrayante annonce d'un mouvement révolutionnaire à Francfort.—Voulez-vous savoir, Madame, l'histoire de cette émeute redoutable? Cela ne vous prendra pas long tems, car la révolution était terminée précisément trois heures et demi après son commencement. C'était assez pour remplir les journaux, effrayer les honnêtes gens, et faire chanter les vauriens. Cependant, tout cela n'était qu'un fracas dans la rue."

We had the pleasure of dining with the British Minister : the party was quite a small one, and I had reason to feel particularly gratified, by the invitation being sent as soon as my card was received, for we were so much birds of passage, that I must otherwise have lost the pleasure of making the acquaintance of one of the most charming women I ever met. Lady C., who is of a German family of high rank, has the appearance, though she has been some years married, of extreme youth ; and her graceful animated manner is that of a young person highly born, and highly educated, full of intelligence and information, but simple and unaffected to perfection. Another charm, which greatly increased my pleasure in conversing with her, was the peculiar and chosen elegance of her English.

She took us a delightful drive to a pretty woodland scene near the town; where, in seasons of peculiar gaiety, and particularly at Easter, the population of Francfort resort, to amuse themselves by smoking, drinking, and dancing in the shade. The *beau monde* on these occasions make it their fashionable drive, and often leave their carriages, to mix with the joyous crowd.

The banks of the Maine have no very noble features here; but they are thickly studded with pretty villas, belonging to the wealthy merchants; and the whole neighbourhood has an air of affluence and comfort. I was amused by the mode of towing vessels up the stream: the horses employed to perform this service are ridden into the middle of the river, when they proceed to draw the flat-bottomed craft after them; sometimes, as it appeared to me, at the risk of drowning both horse and rider.

The public gallery of pictures and casts is a delightful lounge. This institution owes its origin to a splendid bequest from a citizen of the name of Stadel; and the collection has been since greatly augmented at the expense of the town. The building prepared to receive it is so elegantly decorated, that it is itself a beautiful exhibition; and the only fault, if fault it may be called, is, that the beauty of the rooms divides the attention of the spectator, and withdraws the eye too much from the objects they contain. This museum has some very valuable old Flemish pictures, many curious original drawings, and a fine collection of casts from the antique. The picture that pleased me best was the portrait of a burgomaster, by Matsys, bearing date 1482. The finish and life of the head are wonderful. There is also, by Rubens, a child amusing herself with some toy. She is dressed in all the quaint stiffness of Flemish *bon ton,* but certainly looks as nearly alive as it is possible for canvass to do.

It was not till our second visit to this city, on our return from Baden, that I saw its magnificent Burial-Ground. I mention it, however, here, as well as some other objects examined at the same time, that I may not write a chapter upon Francfort with such very glaring omissions.

The British Consul, Mr. K——, who has been a most active and efficient patron of this noble undertaking, had the kindness to show me the plans, and to explain the nature, of the establishment, which greatly increased the interest I felt in seeing it.

If my eye does not greatly deceive me, the new Cemetery of London is very much larger than that of Francfort; but their relative forms are so different, that it is very possible I may be mistaken, at least, as to the degree of their difference in size. Like every other public work of Francfort, its Cemetery is planned upon a noble scale, and handsomely executed; and there are some regulations, which have been enacted respecting the interments in it, which I should rejoice to see adopted with us. But, as I have not the documents before me, I am unwilling to enter too minutely into detail respecting them, from the fear of inaccuracy. The leading principle being, however, as simple as it is admirable, I may state it without any danger of blundering.

Either the company, by whom this noble work has been projected, or the constituted authorities of the city (it matters not which), have taken upon themselves the entire charge of all interments, and the regulation of all the melancholy business connected with the performance of the last offices for the dead. When a citizen expires, notice is given by the family in the proper quarter:—from that moment, every attendance becomes a public instead of a private duty; aud all is performed with that undeviating propriety and exactitude, which can be insured only by the systematic operation of the law. The body is immediately removed to a building erected within the gates of the Cemetery, where it is watched in such a manner, that the slightest indication of returning animation could be instantly perceived;—and, should such a circumstance occur, every contrivance that science has discovered, or art imagined, to assist resuscitation, is at hand to foster it.' In a house, also within the gates of the Cemetery, a physician resides to direct the application of the means employed, and to watch their result. The interment which follows, when every hope of the return of life has passed, is performed with all the reverence and solemnity which the feelings of the surviving friends can desire;—and the expense is fixed at a sum never exceeding *five pounds sterling*, but often falling below it. Not only does this admirable regulation insure to all the solemn performance of a sacred rite, but the last clinging tenderness of human love to the object it has lost, is not made, as elsewhere, to watch, with sickening agony, the hideous approach of the moment that is to part them for ever—nor is it permitted to drain the purse of the poor reckless mourner, who, at such a moment, will rather forget his duty to the living, than omit even the shadow of respect for the dead. I doubt whether the costliest ceremonial that ever was devised, for the interment of the most honoured relics, could produce an effect of so much solemn dignity as this civic care for the dead.

The vaults in which the bodies are deposited, as well as the monuments erected over them, are private property; and they are as simple, or as superb, as individual wealth and taste shall dictate. The enclosure is already adorned by many handsome tombs. One splendid mausoleum, belonging to the family of Bethman, has some very beautiful Italian sculpture, commemorating the loss of a son, who died at Rome.

Close to this Christian burying-ground is another

large area, which has recently been enclosed as a cemetery for the Jews. I did not enter it, but the gateway appeared extremely handsome.

There are so many beautiful and interesting things to be seen at Francfort, that it is very difficult to enumerate them all.—It is a positive *embarras de richesses;* but it would be treason to good taste not to mention the beautiful statue of Ariadne, in the museum of Mr. Bethman. It is said to be the *chef-d'œuvre* of Dennecker, and it is a figure of inconceivable attraction and loveliness. There is, perhaps, rather too much trick in the manner in which it is exhibited ;—the light being thrown upon it through a screen of rose-coloured silk :—and yet it is quarrelling with part of one's pleasure to find fault with this, for it certainly gives a tint of life that increases the beauty. Still, I remembered, as I looked at it, the severe simplicity of the little cabinet containing Somariva's matchless Magdalen, by Canova, and could not but allow that the purer taste was there.

As I had never chanced to enter a Jewish synagogue, I thought I could find no place more favourable for the gratification of the curiosity I felt respecting such an assembly than Francfort. We therefore agreed to join some pleasant friends, who were staying at the Hôtel de Russie, and to proceed together, at six o'clock on a Friday afternoon, to witness the ceremonies, of which I had heard so much, and knew so little. To describe the place we entered would be very difficult. There was a variety and confusion of objects, perfectly defying detail. The building is by no means large, but very lofty. What first strikes the eye, on entering, is the immense multitude of lights—innumerable gilt chandeliers, each one with innumerable branches, were suspended from the roof by richly-wrought iron chains. There was no corner of the building without them: besides these, sconces are thrust into every cranny that can be found to hold them; and enormous candlesticks, exactly in the form in which we see them represented in old Bible engravings, are placed upon the altar. In the midst of the temple is a large, heavy, square elevation, capable of containing about a dozen persons, which was also surrounded on all sides with enormous candlesticks. This illuminated tribune was approached by two flights of steps, and contained seats on three sides of it; the Book of the Law opened upon a desk on the fourth: but no one approached these seats, apparently so distinguished, except some little boys, who amused themselves by running up and down the steps incessantly. In the midst of the ceremonies, a man mounted this tribune, and chanted a few sentences from the open volume. The ladies of our party were shown into an open gallery, but the gentlemen remained below, and obtained seats very near the altar. The gallery had glass windows, which we easily opened, and looked down upon the blaze of light below.

The first ceremony we witnessed was that of a man's changing his round hat for a flat cap. This done, he twisted a white blanket, edged with blue, around him, and chanted from a large volume, in a most inconceivable variety of tones; bowing his head, as he did so, almost incessantly.

At intervals the congregation burst forth into a response:—so loud, so wild, so startling, as almost to cause an emotion of terror.

This response varied in tone, from something approaching a shrill cry to a plaintive wail, the dying cadence of which was occasionally very sweet. The ladies who sat near us in the galleries sometimes appeared earnestly engaged in their devotional exercises—bowing continually and uttering a low chant; and sometimes they chatted together with perfect ease, without even affecting to whisper. Several times during the service the blanket was laid aside by one and taken by another; and once by a lad, apparently about fourteen, who retained his little *casquette* on his head while he read, or rather chanted, some portion of the Scriptures, which lay upon the altar. There is one feature, so peculiar and so prominent, that I cannot avoid mentioning it: this is the uncleansed state of the building. If I might make such a distinction, I should say that it was not dirty; I mean that no objects of accidental disgust contributed to its extraordinary condition: but it seemed as if the dust of the temple were held sacred; for there is no part of the building, walls, ceiling, floor, steps, nor any object within it, that is not covered, nay, loaded, with a mass of heavy, accumulated, long-settled dust. The vast number of handsome gilt chandeliers and candlesticks would have a splendid appearance, were they not thus veiled in this universal drapery of black, stifling dust and cobweb.

I was disappointed at hearing no music,—for certainly none of the sounds I heard deserve the name,—and I had entered with ideas of Hebrew melodies floating in my fancy. I asked a lady near me, if music made no part of their service, and I almost expected she would answer—"As for our harps, we have hung them up upon the trees;" but she only replied, "Quelquefois nous avons encore des meilleures voix."

I must by no means forget to mention the very courteous civility which was shown to us by every one we approached. Each lady, as she entered the gallery, smiled and bowed to us, as if we had been her especial guests; and the gentlemen told us they were treated with the same politeness below. Baron Rothschild was present there; and I afterwards learnt from a gentleman of the city, who knew him well, that his religious observances were peculiarly severe. He said that, at particular seasons, long fastings were enjoined in the synagogue;

and that, on these occasions, this gentleman had been known to remain in the temple for eighteen hours together, and had more than once been carried home in a state of complete exhaustion.

We obtained permission to see the Baron's pretty villa, which is about a mile from the town;—or rather the gardens belonging to it, for the house is not shown. These gardens are not at all superb; but they are nicely kept, and show an abundance of fine flowers. As we approached the entrance, we met a very gentleman-like looking personage leaving the gates in a handsome carriage; and our coachman informed us this was the Baron's *Master of the Horse.*

At our second visit, we again passed a Sunday at Francfort, and once more visited the beautiful new church. I thought, as I looked at its majestic simplicity of style, and listened to the glorious hymn ringing round its dome, that Luther himself might look down upon it with complacency. This great reformer's name is still spoken of among the people, as freshly as if the benefits he had conferred on them were of yesterday.

"Luther was a greater man than Napoleon," said a citizen of Francfort, who sat by me at the table-d'hôte, "and his new rule will be longer felt than the famous code of the other; though that was worth something too."

I heard another German remark, that, in travelling through the country, he would undertake to tell, on entering a village, whether it were Protestant or Catholic. "The Protestants," said he, "are always *better off*—they have not so many fêtes and festivals to make them idle."

We enjoyed another Sunday opera on our return, and on this occasion were so fortunate as to hear Madame Fischer Achten. She is by far the most accomplished singer I have heard in this country. The performance was Sargino, by Paer, and much of the music is delightful. I hope to hear Madame Fischer again at the Haymarket.

Among the many proofs of obliging hospitality afforded to strangers, is that of admission to the Cassino. A stranger's ticket is easily obtained; and the bearer of it has the full privileges of a subscriber for one month. I availed myself of the permission granted me to walk into the reading-rooms, which are very commodious, and well-furnished with books, pamphlets, &c. The large table was covered with polyglot collection of newspapers. In casting my eyes upon a French one amongst them, I was amused by the following literal translation of a modern political phrase:—" Il y a tout lieu de croire que le Roi d'Angleterre refusera la démission des Ministres, et consentira à une FOURNÉE de pairs."

Before leaving Francfort, I took the liberty of requesting permission to wait upon her Royal Highness the Landgravine of Hesse Hombourg, which was most kindly granted. Her Highness's beautiful residence is about two hours' drive from the city; and even if it had not the interest of being the abode of a Princess of England, it well deserves to be visited.

The town of Francfort is situated on a plain, the extent of which, at least in the direction of Hombourg, almost marks its territory: for, after passing by one of the old towers, which stand like sentinels round its limits, the country gradually rises; and the town of Hombourg is situated on a beautiful elevation, which seems to rise on purpose to look out upon the noble line of the Taunus hills, and down upon the lovely valley which stretches towards them.

The residence of our amiable Princess is just what a loyal English subject would wish to see it;— noble in style and dimension, beautiful as to its site and the country which surrounds it, and adorned throughout with that exquisite finish of perfect comfort, which perhaps only an English princess would require, and which certainly no other could so well succeed in bringing about her.

The Princess had returned only a few days before from Hanover, and spoke with great enthusiasm of the beauty of the scenery through which she had travelled. "I can never forget Windsor and Richmond," said her Royal Highness, " but Germany is a glorious country!" With the condescending good-humour for which she has always been distinguished, she herself led us through the noble suite of rooms that look towards the richly-wooded ridge of the Taunus hills, or mountains, as we should certainly call them in England. The view from these rooms is superb.

The road leading to the castle, though very steep, had not prepared me for the bold declivity on the other side, over which this range of apartments looks. The gardens of the palace lie at its feet, and the whole scene is one of great beauty and magnificence. It was with true English spirit that her Royal Highness showed us her noble library. "I brought these volumes from England with me," she said; adding, with a smile, "I am proud of my library"—and she might well be so, for not only does it contain a very large and excellent collection of books, but every thing in the room announces it to be the favourite retreat of a person of literary habits and refined taste. It is the only room that I saw in Germany at all in the same style. There are many in which books are found in abundance, but I saw none so calculated for the elegant indulgence of literary leisure. Yet it appeared that all the hours of reading were not spent here, for I think there was scarcely one of the apartments, in the fine suite which we saw, that had not books in it by some contrivance or other. Sometimes there was an elegant little table with a row of volumes forming the back of it—sometimes a small portable case, just large enough to contain a set of miniature favourites; and in one room filled with all kinds of pretty things, the whole space below the hangings is lined with a wainscoting of books.

In many of the rooms are portraits, some of them very fine ones, of the Royal Family of England. I stopped before one of George the Third, being struck by the powerful likeness: "You know that portrait?" said the Princess; "It is my father —it is quite perfect."

After this gratifying visit, we drove to an hotel at Hombourg, where we ordered dinner; and, both before and after this repast, amused ourselves by exploring the beautiful environs of the town.

As the gentlemen were disposed after dinner to take a longer walk up the hills than I liked to venture upon, I returned alone to the hotel, scribbled in my note-book, and took coffee while they proceeded. I will therefore give my son's account of this walk, as being much more satisfactory than my own.

"A road, as straight as the flight of an arrow, leads from Hombourg to the top of one of the Taunus range, and the view from this point is very fine, looking over the whole of the Francfort plain, or valley of the Maine, to where the hills of the Black Forest close it in on the opposite side. The greatest part of the Taunus is lime, with large and frequent veins of quartz, sometimes very white and pure, and sometimes containing iron. The summits are a chaos of broken rocks, without any soil between them : some of the blocks are of an enormous size, and it can hardly be doubted that the state in which they lie is the consequence of some violent commotion of the earth. If I might be allowed a theory, I would say that, at the time the volcanic matter at the Siebengebirge, Rolandseck, and Unkel burst through the slate stratum, these rocks were dashed by the same convulsion into the fragments which we here find scattered around in all directions. The dip of the slate stratum, always from north to south, certainly seems to favour this wild hypothesis.

"I would advise every one who visits Francfort

to spend a day or two,—a week would not be too much,—at Hombourg. I know no place where there are so many delightful excursions in the environs, and so many enchanting views within reach of a lady's walk or ride—such forests to wander in, such hills to climb. On the side by which we quitted the town, the woods have been most tastefully laid out in walks and drives, so as to make the forest both safe and easy of access; and yet it has been done without at all injuring the romantic beauty of the scene. The singular part of the arrangement is, that the different kinds of scenery are made to blend, or rather to follow each other, so artfully, that it is difficult to say where one ends and the other begins. On leaving the town we came to 'gardens trim' and well laid out with gravel walks and terraces; from gardens we came to groves, from groves to woods, still getting wilder and wilder, as we advanced; the paths becoming narrower and less frequent, the shade thicker and darker, till here and there a mass of rock appears, and the woodland scene becomes a forest. What seemed the gentle slope of a hill, now grew to be the steep side of a mountain, till at length we found ourselves in the midst of crags and leaping waterfalls, in a mountainous wilderness, wild enough for the most romantic spirit to revel in, and this without being conscious where the different changes had taken place.

"We had not long entered the forest when we roused a fine doe from a thicket close by. We saw a variety of game here,—deer, hares, and pheasants. On one side of the straight road I have mentioned, there is a beautiful, well-fenced park, belonging, I presume, to the Landgravine, which seemed to be well stocked with deer. Just as we came to the palace-gardens, on our return, we met the Princess going out on an evening drive among her lovely groves and noble hills."

Chapter X.

Darmstadt—Heppenheim—Storkenberg—Bergstrasse—Weinheim—Peasantry—Crops—Mannheim—The Palace—Ducal Gardens—Ball—Observatory—Church of the Jesuits—Theatre—Schwetzingen Gardens.

From Francfort we proceeded to Darmstadt,—a little capital which, not long ago, was celebrated as that of good King René for music, dance, and song; but it lost much in losing its late Grand Duke. His garden of pleasaunce, his stately manège, his delightful Opera, are all, if not fallen to decay, at least fallen into disuse; and the place, notwithstanding the noble air of its spacious mansions, with their ample gardens and gay verandahs, looks like a city whose glory has passed away. The late sovereign appears to have been the centre around which all that was gay and courtly moved; and the mourning draperies put up to honour his obsequies seem still to hang about the objects he loved best. His darling Opera is hushed and silent;—weeds contest the soil with the flowers of his garden;—and in the streets of his pretty capital too much grass is growing to permit it to look either gay or flourishing.

Nevertheless, I advise all travellers to proceed from Francfort to Mannheim by the way of Darmstadt, instead of turning back to Mayence, and going on by the river. Having tried both routes, I feel privileged to give counsel in the case, and can testify, not only that there is very little interest or beauty in the voyage between Mayence and Mannheim, but that the drive from Darmstadt is through some of the loveliest scenery of the country. It is true, indeed, that the steam-boat passes by the venerable city of Worms, but all which can be seen of it from the deck is not enough to induce a change of route.

We made this delightful little journey in an open carriage; but even so, I could by no means see as much as I wished, and therefore determined, though at the risk of arriving late at the place of our destination, to climb one of the castled hills, at the feet of which we were passing. For this purpose we left the carriage for an hour or two at Heppenheim, and indulged in one of those delightful rambles, of which I enjoyed many during our tour, and which showed more of the characteristic features of the country, and of its wild and peculiar beauty, than can be conceived by merely looking at the various celebrated spots seen from the high road of the Rhine.

The little town of Heppenheim itself has much that is interesting: its high antiquity is proved by a stone in the church bearing date 805; it has, moreover, considerable claims to picturesque beauty, from the bright ripple of its pretty brook, its uncouth bridges, and its ruinous walls. We hardly took a step after leaving the inn that did not bring us to a picture. Little urchins, with one scanty garment as the only covering to their rosy limbs, were dabbling under the shade of one green bridge; and a beautiful girl, with golden hair and bare legs, was carrying flowery fodder to her cow, over another; while at the low, wicketed door of many a Teniers-like cottage, were groupes which would have made an admirable study for Wilkie.

After a lingering walk through the town, we mounted, mounted, mounted, by a long, sinuous path among the vines, till we reached the majestic ruins of Storkenberg. I wish that the barons who built, and dwelt in, these glorious old castles had not left such reputations for tyranny, cruelty, and all that is hateful, behind them; for there is something so noble in the choice of their commanding sites, that it is difficult not to feel respect for the daring spirits who, planting a foot upon these towering heights, exclaimed, " Here shall be my stronghold and my home!"

Having conquered this steep ascent, spite of a flinty path beneath our feet, and a scorching sun above our heads, we sat down in the shade of a mighty wall, and fully enjoyed the recompense of our toil. The view from the Storkenberg is made up of all that the eye best loves to look upon. Hill and valley, forest and fertile plain, rocks, ruins, lowly hamlets, and knightly castles, all are spread out before the sight, with such lavish prodigality of beauty, as might well suffice to furnish forth a dozen landscapes. Behind us the hill sunk but a little, ere it rose again into a mountain forest; —so dark and wild, and yet so lovely, in the contrast its shade offered to the sunny hill we were about to descend, that it was only by an effort of great prudence that I was enabled to refuse my consent to plunging into it. The spot on which we reposed was, however, well calculated to make us forget our fatigue. The shade was perfect, and a delightful breeze seemed to ascend to us from the valley. It is really a woful thing to turn from such a spot, and know that it is resigned for ever; for who can hope a second time to be favoured by all the little intricate contingencies which must be strung together, all in the right order, before one can find oneself on the rocky summit of the distant Storkenberg? But the day was waning fast, and reluctantly leaving our delightful lair, we traced back our way, peeping over the luxuriant growth of the vines, till we again found ourselves beside the brook of Heppenheim.

We got some excellent coffee at the little inn, and then proceeded along the Bergstrasse, as the magnificent range of hills is called, among which this fine road passes. Every moment of our progress showed us new and increasing splendour of scenery, till we reached the wondrous little town of Weinheim.

I shall make no attempt to describe the situation of this place, as singular as it is beautiful, for I am quite sure I could not make myself intelligible. We saw it, too, when the setting sun gives that breadth of shadow and power of light to a bold and hilly landscape, which is so utterly beyond the power of words to record. We here again left the carriage, and spent more time than our driver willingly allowed, in running from point to point, to gaze upon the plain below us, through which the broad Rhine swept along; and then upon the wild peaks of the Bergstrasse on the other side, which, lovelier far in the near distinctness of their dark forests, and their granite crags, seemed to make the distant Vosges look like a thin mass of vapour on the horizon.

Let no one, who has time to spare, content himself with seeing the country between Darmstadt and Mannheim, merely in the course of a long day's short journey, as we did; but, let him, after taking up his quarters at the latter place, devote one entire day to Weinheim. The high antiquity and bold position of its walls and towers, as well as the exceeding beauty of the landscape over which they hang, render it a spot of very peculiar interest.

It was not till after our cautious driver had repeatedly told us we should be very late at Mannheim, that we at length remounted the carriage to follow the road, which we saw, but too plainly, must immediately take us out of sight of all that had so greatly delighted us. A rapid descent soon brought us to the plain on which Mannheim is situated, and the coming darkness appeared likely to hide nothing from us, more than a continuation of rich and ripening crops. This valley is cultivated in long narrow strips, without any enclosures. We saw wheat, hops, potatoes, flax, hemp, oats, rye, clover, Indian corn, and tobacco. There are also some patches of vines, but these are in small quantity here, being chiefly cultivated on the southern sides of the steepest hills;—a situation which at once shelters them from the biting north, and gives all the sunshine of the climate, doubled by reflection. I was surprised to find such fine crops of Indian corn. Though it does not grow quite so high as I have seen it in America, it appears to flourish, and bears a large and heavy ear.

Independent of the beautiful scenery of the Bergstrasse, the road we had this day travelled was more than commonly interesting from the picturesque dress of the numerous peasantry scattered on and about it. It was the last week in July, and harvest of every kind, except that of the vineyards, was near at hand. All the rustic population seemed in activity, and there really appeared no end to the pretty variety of figures that peopled the landscape. Old men and women, young men and maidens, frolicsome boys and laughing girls, all in the strange, fantastic dresses of the country, thronged the fields. The costume of the women was very pretty—large white sleeves, pushed high above the elbow, coloured bodices, and full, short petticoats, with the hair sometimes fastened up in a net, and sometimes plaited in long braids, as the girls of Switzerland wear it. A few among them had enormously large straw hats, but these were much less frequent here, than we found them afterwards towards Baden. The men, too, all looked like pictures out of a book of fancy dresses; with their large cocked hats, long straight-breasted coats, and showy waistcoats. The general effect was very much that of the *corps de ballet* in a rustic dance at the French Opera.

According to the prediction of our driver, we did not reach Mannheim till long after night-fall. The streets appeared long and wide, but very dark; an occasional candle on the counter of a druggist's shop, or from the yet open window of a private dwelling, being all the light we saw.

On reaching the principal hotel, however, every window of its wide extent seemed illuminated; and we received, in answer to our application for apartments, the reply that might have been expected, "Every room in the house is occupied."

These are unpleasant sounds to hear at eleven o'clock at night;—and, as we had received no direction to any second inn, we remained for a moment quite at a loss to determine what we were to do next. On perceiving this, a waiter again stepped forward, and begged to recommend us to the Weinberg. We gladly followed the direction, and in a few minutes found ourselves as perfectly comfortable, and as completely at home, as it was possible for an hotel to make us.

I have seldom seen so large a town as Mannheim with so few people moving about it; and yet there is no appearance of desolation either. Everything looks handsome, neat, and cheerful. There are well-dressed ladies and gentlemen walking in the streets; and pretty *soubrettes*, with hair as nicely arranged as if they were going to a ball, tripping with dainty baskets on their arms, to do their ladies' bidding. Then there are soldiers enough to make it look military, and music enough to make it seem gay; but all is so orderly and quiet, and has an air of such *point-device* neatness, that it seems as if there were some officer in the town whose duty it was to go through the streets every morning, to see that all things were put in order; the nice little fruit-stalls in their proper places; and all the tidy little boys whipping their tops just in the right corner, and nowhere else. The whole appearance of the town points it out as a princely residence; but the present Grand Duke of Baden has fixed his abode at Carlsruhe; and some apartments, only, in the magnificent palace at Mannheim, are inhabited by the Dowager Grand Duchess Stephanie.

In elegance of arrangement and decoration, I have seen nothing to compare with the Prince of Orange's palace at Brussels; but, in size, it is a plaything compared to that of Mannheim. One wing of this immense fabric was destroyed by fire, when in possession of the French in 1795, by the bombardment of the Austrians; and, till informed that it had contained the theatre, I felt quite at a loss to imagine to what purpose it could have been applied; every requisite for a princely residence being so amply furnished by the other parts. Besides rooms for state, and rooms for comfort, almost innumerable, this vast pile contains a very extensive suite of apartments fitted up as a picture gallery, another for antiques, and another for books. In addition to all this, there appear to be numerous suites, appropriated as residences for persons of distinction holding places about the court; and very charming residences they must be, many of them looking over the superb gardens to the Rhine, and the fine chain of mountains beyond it.

There is also a large and handsome chapel, making part of the remaining wing; and more colonnades, galleries, corridors, and staircases, than would suffice for half a dozen palaces in these degenerate days. That part of the residence, which has been recently fitted up for the Dowager Grand Duchess, is rich and elegant in its furniture and hangings; but it bears about the same proportion to the entire edifice, that the private apartments of the Queen of England do to the whole of Windsor Castle. The fine gardens, which reach from the palace to the Rhine, are admirably laid out *à l'Anglaise;* and, like those of all the other sovereign princes of Germany, are open to the public. This indulgence is repaid by the most cautious and respectful forbearance from all injury, on the part of the people; all the beautiful variety of shrubs and forest trees, so profusely scattered over the grounds, still sweep the lawns with their luxuriant branches, and evidently can never have been touched by any wanton or mischievous hand.

These noble grounds are bounded towards the river by a terrace, affording one of the finest walks imaginable. The Rhine, and the fertile valley beyond it, with the wavy outline of the Bergstrasse, are on one side; the gardens, the palace, the towers of the church and observatory, with Mont Tonnerre for a background, on the other.

The unfettered privilege of entering at all hours among such groves and lawns, such shrubs and flowers, would be delightful to any people; but must, I think, be very peculiarly so to the Germans, whose passion for flowers is as universal, and as evident, as their love of music. Not a cottage but has its sweet-scented *parterre;* not a hut but can show some little morsel of earth, if it be only a yard square, fenced about with broken platters, and fragments of old tubs, yet containing delicious blossoms, cultivated with a degree of care, and science too, that would not disgrace the King's

Road between Chelsea and Fulham. This love of flowers is equally perceptible in town and country; and I think it would be difficult to find a house in which some balcony or window did not give a proof of it.

There are so many pleasant excursions within a morning's drive of Mannheim, that I should have much liked to have passed a week there; but unfortunately we had not the advantage of knowing a single person in the town. I brought a letter of introduction, which would have been sufficient to do all I wished for us, in the way of presentation, but *par malheur*, the individual to whom it was addressed had left Mannheim for the summer; and nothing remained for us, but to see what was most interesting in the place, and depart. Having decided that less than two days could not suffice, even for this, we inquired of our host what public amusements were going on, that might occupy the two evenings we proposed to stay. "There is a ball to-night, and a play to-morrow," was the answer received; and we rejoiced at our good fortune, for neither of these was of daily occurrence.

I was rather surprised, however, upon making inquiries respecting a carriage to convey us to this ball, at being assured that I should have no need of one, for that all the world walked to the Muhlau, and that it was "*une promenade enchanteresse.*"

The weather was, indeed, such as to make an evening walk far from disagreeable. The heat throughout the day had been oppressive, but we had now a cool breeze and a bright moon; and we set off, nothing loth, for the Muhlau. The room is very plain, but of good size and shape for waltzing. It was already nearly full; but, with the civility, or rather kindness, which is so remarkable a feature in the manners of this country, we were ushered, as strangers, to the top of the room, and obtained good places for seeing the dancing.

But, though beauty was abundant, and though nothing was to be found fault with in the general neatness of dress and appearance, it was immediately evident that this was not the sort of meeting we had expected; and, on making subsequent inquiries, we found that two balls in the week were held throughout the season:—the one being for the noblesse, and the other for the bourgeoisie :—we were at the latter.

Though we might, perhaps, have preferred seeing how noble ladies performed the dance which is native to them, and which is engrafting itself slowly, but surely, on our own manners, we had, nevertheless, much to console us for the disappointment; for never did I see two hundred people met together, who had more completely the air of enjoying themselves.

For my own particular share of the amusement, I found a study that would have lasted me longer than the time we stayed, without any danger that I should grow weary of it. Close to the place where we had stationed ourselves was a group of females: consisting, I think, of two families, for there were two matronly women seated together, and four young girls, who, when not dancing, constantly returned to stand near them. Three of these were certainly sisters; the other was perhaps a cousin or a friend, or an acquaintance; but it was clear that they had joined parties for the evening. The three sisters might have served as models, if not for the Graces, at least for Hebe; or any other goddess or nymph that should be represented as the personification of prettiness, health, and gaiety—fresh, fair, light-haired, bright-eyed beings, who looked as if they had nothing to do but to dance through life, throwing flowers and smiles about them as they went on. The solitary girl was a little yellow creature, with an undeniable pug nose; and, if her teeth were white, she had certainly no business with so extremely wide a mouth to display them. But this yellow little creature had a pair of eyes—such eyes! I might be able to describe them better had it been possible to look at them steadily for two minutes together;—but they sparkled, and shot, and darted about their glances at such a rate, that nobody could look full at them without winking. All, therefore, that I can positively say respecting these marvellous eyes is, that they were black, with lashes which, when she was merciful enough to look down, seemed to throw her face into shade. Her hair was black, too, parted upon her forehead, and just put behind her ears without any care or skill whatever; while one large knot collected the remainder of her neglected tresses at the back of her head. Her dress, too, was far unlike that of her fair companions. They were habited in delicate white muslin; while this strange little creature chose to show off her tawny complexion by wearing a plain, dark frock, of very ordinary materials, and without the slightest attempt at ornament of any kind.

Such was the party placed next to us; and they were surrounded by the smartest-looking young men in the room;—one, two, three,—I reckoned seven;—who approached in succession before the dancing began. The blue-eyed beauties knew them all, for they smiled and nodded. The yellow girl knew them, too; but instead of smiling, she poked up her brown shoulder at most of them, and talked assiduously to her mother; nevertheless, every one of them asked her to dance. Having promised the first, she shook her head without speaking, in reply to all the others, and appeared to take very little notice of any of them.

At length the waltz began. The three beauties

got partners, too, and all darted off into the whirling circle together. When they came back again, the same scene was repeated, nay, worse, for even the partners of the fair girls would only talk to the brown one. I never watched such witchery. It was a single word, a single syllable, perhaps, that she carelessly bestowed on each; but the gipsy had some fascination about her that seemed to be irresistible;—and she knew it; for she played her tricks and threw her glances with so much wilful mischief, that her pretty companions looked vexed, and their mother enraged, at her monopolizing proceedings.

How much longer I could have found amusement from watching her vagaries I know not; for we were chased away by the performance of an operation which might, perhaps, when completed, conduce to the comfort of the dancers; if they lost not all inclination for the exercise, while it was going on. A considerable portion of dust having been disengaged from the floor by an hour's incessant beating, returned to it again, while the two hundred waltzers reposed for a short space.

During this interval, two stout women made their appearance, bearing between them a huge, heavy carpet or rug, dripping with water, which, on reaching the top of the room, they let fall on the floor; each of them still retaining a corner of it, and separating from each other as far as its size would permit them. In this fashion they ran the whole length of the ball-room, dragging the wet rug after them to the bottom of it, when they immersed it afresh in a pail of water, and prepared to repeat the operation.

Both the performance and the performers were too uncouth to be agreeable; and, moreover, the union of the dust and the water produced so very disagreeable an effect upon the air, that we left the room directly.

The banks of the Necker near Mannheim, where it joins the Rhine, have no very striking features; but the gradual approaching of the two rivers, as seen from the observatory, is very interesting. The entire view from this point is indeed magnificent, extending over the whole country between the Bergstrasse and the Vosges;—but, if it commanded no other prospect than the various roofs of the palace, it would be worth mounting to the top, for the sole purpose of seeing their whole extent at a glance.

Near that wing of the building which has been destroyed by fire is a large convent, formerly occupied by a powerful community of Jesuits. On one side it is connected with the palace, by means of a chamber of communication still existing over a gateway leading into the gardens: and on the other with the magnificent church built by the community, assisted, however, by many noble donations from the princes of Baden. We entered this old convent, the painted staircase of which still retains some traces of its former dignity; but the building is now chiefly occupied by schools, and has little left in its appearance that tells of the splendour for which it was once distinguished. The church, however, is unchanged; and it is not difficult to trace in its gorgeous ornaments both the taste and the wealth of its founders. The altar in particular is well worthy a close examination;—it is constructed of the most costly marbles, and the pillars of the ark that stands upon it are of fine agate. The whole aspect of this church, though immeasurably inferior in all respects to the glorious cathedrals of former ages, has that about it which strongly awakens interest. Its peculiar arrangement, as connected with the palace and the convent, vividly recalls the days when princes and priests felt mutual dependence and mutual reverence. The abbot passed from his convent to the presence of his sovereign through a private room, unchallenged and unannounced, to be consulted on the prince's political anxieties, and to afford him the comfort and assistance of his advice. The sovereign, by the same route, could enter the cell of his confessor, and pass thence with the sacred privacy of devotion into the chamber, which is still to be seen, enclosed by windows, above the altar.

That for purposes such as these the palace, convent, and church were constructed in the manner we now see them cannot be doubted. Such intimate communion is now no longer needed; but, perhaps, it requires the test of longer experience than has yet been given it, before the advantages to be derived from withdrawing the voices of churchmen from the councils of the state shall be clearly ascertained.

Our second evening was spent at the theatre, which is large and handsome. It was extremely well filled, and the company had the same air of feeling themselves at home as at Francfort. The alley in the pit, immediately below the boxes, was filled by very gentlemanlike-looking men, most of whom were officers. They remained standing during the whole performance; and between the acts took advantage of their position to converse with the ladies in the boxes. Here we saw two pieces performed; but both were so short, that the curtain dropped upon the lamps before daylight had quite disappeared.

The least agreeable features in Mannheim are its waterless fountains. These are, I think, six in number: they are built of marble, and very nobly conceived; but it seems that the Grand Duke, who projected this beautiful and useful embellishment of the city, died before the water was conveyed to them, and in this abortive state they have remained ever since.

From Mannheim we drove to Schwetzingen, for the purpose of seeing the celebrated gardens there; second only, it is said, to those of the Elector of Hesse Cassel, at Wilhelmshohe. They are, indeed, truly magnificent; and on so much more vast a scale than anything of the kind in England, that I know not to what I may compare them.

Were I to enumerate the terraces, fountains, aviaries, temples, waterfalls, grottos, groves, parterres, lawns, lakes, statues, mosques, baths, boats, and bridges, with which they are studded, I should delude the reader into a belief that it was a crowded collection of incongruous objects; but this is very far from being the case. The space they occupy is a hundred and seventy acres; and this, by the skilful arrangement of the artist who laid them out, is made amply sufficient to present all these pretty things in succession, without unpleasantly interfering with each other.

Some of the sculptured groups are sufficiently good to produce an excellent effect, and the magnificence of the trees among which they are seen, the stately length of the noble avenues, the judicious mixture of water in the landscape, and the wonderful variety and extent of the walks leading through it, altogether make these ducal gardens an exhibition that no one should neglect to visit.

Among the gratifications offered by this now forsaken residence, is a theatre for private performances, which, some years ago, were carried on with great spirit by the court. It has pit, boxes, orchestra, scenes, and so on, in very good style; with the additional advantage of opening at the extremity of the stage upon a grove of trees, whenever the piece performed would permit such a decoration. At another spot in the grounds there was a prettier theatre still, in which a raised terrace of turf made the boxes, a well-shorn lawn the pit, a bright cascade, surrounded by statues, the back scene; while roses and honeysuckles, trained upon trellis-work, constituted the side scenes. Here, as the gardener informed us, plays were frequently performed by noble lords and ladies during the summer, as well as at the less airy theatre; and to both the public were freely admitted, some of the best places being courteously reserved for strangers. There is something exceedingly noble in the arrangements of these German princes, as to their places of recreation : everything is upon a scale of great magnificence, and the public are admitted to so large a share of the enjoyment, that it may well be supposed every amusement prepared for the prince must increase his popularity with the people.

A large suite of banqueting and withdrawing-rooms show a fine façade to the gardens on one side of the palace; and an orangery and conservatory, ending in the theatre, answer to it on the other. The flowers retain possession of their noble habitation, but all the rest of the dwelling, including the chapel, has a most desolate aspect.

There are, in truth, so many splendid palaces belonging to the Grand Duke of Baden, that it would be equally useless and troublesome to keep them all up as residences. To maintain their extensive gardens in the style in which they are always kept, must require a very considerable revenue; yet this appears to be done at all of them;

the motive for which may be, that the neighbourhood of each should suffer as little as possible from the absence of the sovereign.

We dined, not too well, at one of the little inns in the village of Schwetzingen, and then proceeded to Heidelberg.

Chapter XI.

Heidelberg — Neuenheim — Heidelberg Castle — The Necker—Neckersteinach—Tilsberg—Steinach—Tun of Heidelberg—Broken Tower—English Antiquaries.

HEIDELBERG is placed at the point where the Necker emerges from the narrow valley through which it has run from its source, and whence it flows through a flat rich plain, till it joins the Rhine at Mannheim. At the entrance of this narrow valley, hills, or rather mountains, covered with dark forests, rise suddenly from the water's edge on either side, and you are again in the midst of the wild heights of the Bergstrasse. Between these, after passing the town of Heidelberg, there is just room enough for the stream to pass, with a road on each side of it. Here and there, indeed, a hollow recess gives space for a little villa, with its hanging garden; and on the left, as you ascend the river, a few vines find room to grow; but these often give place to rocks with their frequent quarries.

It is on the right-hand height that the majestic ruins of Heidelberg Castle hang in mid-air. These are opened to the eye, on entering the town from Schwetzingen, with a degree of splendour quite unequalled by any other view in the country. The evening was closing as we drove up to our hotel, but we all agreed that it was impossible to sleep till we had penetrated to the centre of this enormous pile. Having given a hasty glance at the apartments, and ordered coffee to be ready in an hour, we set off. But more than two elapsed ere we returned; and, even then, darkness had driven us from the walls before one-half of this extraordinary fabric had been even looked at.

I would I had power to describe all we saw through those hours of twilight, but there is a twofold difficulty in the attempt. On the one-hand, I might disgust the reader by a high-flown rhapsody of admiration; and, on the other, I should be sure to vex myself by the tame and flat insufficiency of any praise I could bestow.

Though the ascent is steep, the road has been made almost easy, by the care bestowed upon it.

The first steep, straight portion of it, however, has no beauty; but, having mastered this, your reward awaits you. From this point, there are two approaches to the castle; one, by a fair, smooth path, sheltered by noble trees, and gradually leading above the tops of those which grow on the hillside, till at length the level space behind the castle and in front of the great gateway is reached; the other is by a steep flight of steps into the very heart of the fortress, through a vast, subterranean, vaulted hall, which conducts you to a small interior court, and thence by another flight to the level of the court-yard. Take which route you will, there is no danger of the highest wrought expectations being disappointed. By the first, you will wind round the base of towers, which look as if a giant architect had reared them for a giant prince;—by the last, you will be led under arches which, even in ruin, seem to speak of eternal duration:—and both lead to a terrace, from whence a view is seen, so much beyond what the power of words can paint, that all the most faithful traveller can say, to any purpose, on the subject, is, "Go, all, with as little delay as possible, and look at it."

On our first visit, we followed the more circuitous route under the trees. Had we not done so, we should have been quickly involved in almost total darkness; for, even at mid-day, but little light finds its way into the subterranean hall.

On reaching the esplanade, before the chief entrance, you have no very extended view; for the lofty summit of the Geissberg is on one side, and the wide-spreading castle on the other; but, on passing under this portal, and crossing the courtyard, you reach another archway, which leads to the grand north terrace, acknowledged to be one of the finest points of view in Europe. The very last glories of sunset were fading from the summit of the Vosges, as we reached it; and all below this gigantic terrace was already in the deepest shade. The Necker, alone, still reflected the faint remnant of daylight; but, on the opposite side, the towering Heiligenberg was as black as night. On the terrace, however, we remained—not planet-struck, but prospect-struck—till we could see no longer; and then we found our way back as we could, through the darkness of the arched gateways, and under the scarcely lighter shadow of the fine trees, which hung over the walk leading down to the town.

The following morning it was decided, that, before mounting again to the castle, we should cross the bridge over the Necker, and look at it from a distance. The view from the opposite side of the river is very beautiful; but the castle itself loses somewhat of its magical effect, by being seen completely against the hill which rises behind it. Unlike all the other ruins I have seen, Heidelberg owes not its greatest beauty to decay. There are many parts of it, in which the architectural splendour of the building still remains sufficiently entire to render it an object of universal admiration; independently of its superb position and great historical interest. In fact, the most valuable drawings that have been made of it, are by no means picturesque, but entirely architectural. The scenery around it, of a style the most grand and wild, is hardly within reach of the pencil. If attempted from the heights, all the enchantment vanishes; for a map-like sort of bird's-eye view is all which can be hoped for. If taken from below, the great object of the attempt, the glorious castle, is seen flat against the dark, uniform background of the Geissberg hill; and neither light, air, nor effect can be hoped for. In short, Heidelberg is a place calculated to put a landscape painter in a fever; for, while it surrounds him with all he must most wish to have, it shows him, at the same time, that little of it is within his reach.

The village of Neuenheim, on this side of the river, has many interesting features. We were shown a roof,—a very humble one, which is said to have sheltered Luther, on his retreat from Worms, after meeting the Convocation assembled there in 1521, by order of Charles V. Two windows are pointed out as being those of the chamber which he occupied. There is a very tempting walk, called the "*Sentier des Philosophes*," that leads from the village to the top of the Heiligenberg; and, had such a path, to such a mountain, met me anywhere else, I should certainly have followed it,—whatever the risk of fatigue might have been;—but, now, the great magnet drew us back again across the bridge;

and once more we prepared to mount to the castle. We were accosted, on our route, by numberless little boys, who petitioned for the honour of serving us as guides amid the ruins. Their mode of address was very engaging; for they uniformly prefaced the request by presenting to each of us a pretty nosegay of freshly-gathered flowers, out of the little baskets with which they were furnished, apparently as a sort of professional property. We selected a fine bright-looking little fellow, who performed the office admirably; and, under his guidance, we now traversed the whole of this amazing fabric. I will not venture to inflict upon my readers any attempt of mine to recount its vast, complicated, intricate, and most splendid varieties. All I can do is to record our delight, our wonder, our intense feeling of astonishment at the marvels, both of art and nature, so lavishly spread before us. This enormous pile, the work of successive princes, through many ages, is a relic of what was most gorgeous and most noble in each.

Towers and battlements, statues and columns, with " storied architrave," and sculptured frieze,—

the banqueting-hall, and the chapel,—all stood before us, almost appalling in their stateliness—yet all slowly crumbling into irretrievable decay. On turning from this scene to the still fresh beauty of the landscape below,—to the town, the river, the valley,—over which the lordly dwelling had so long towered, pre-eminent in dignity, as in place, the whole effect is so magnificent, that it is impossible to contemplate it without strong emotion.

I heartily wish to avoid, if possible, the writing descriptions in *issimo*, as Lord Orford calls it, but sometimes it is very difficult to do this; and, spite of all the caution I have endeavoured to use, I almost fear whether I may not already have offended against the modesty of common sense, while speaking of this extraordinary scene.

The remainder of a long morning was spent upon the Geissberg. After visiting every part of the ruins, and deciding that we would pass one entire day amongst them, before we left Heidelberg, we proceeded to the fine gardens, the lawns and terraces of which cling to the side of the mountain all round the castle. To the summit of this mountain we then ascended, and sought, in vain, for some traces of the original tower, said to have existed before the present magnificent edifice was built upon the lower elevation of the Jettenbuhl. There are many wild legends circulated respecting it; some of which speak of a beautiful sorceress, named Jetta, who was its inhabitant; and who, before a stone of the present castle was laid, prophesied its foundation, its greatness, its long-increasing splendour, the glories of its founder's race, (now on the throne of Bavaria,) its awful trembling, when repeatedly struck by thunderbolts from heaven, and its subsequent slow and lingering decay into the elements, from which her voice had called it. But, though we failed to find the fragments of moss-covered stones, which they told us still remained in the depth of the woods, we came upon the Wolfsbrun, —a small stream, on the brink of which the sorceress Jetta was slain by a wolf, immediately after she had uttered the prophecy above-mentioned. It is a spot which a poet might draw upon for ever, for his woodland imagery.

In the evening, we took a circuit of the town;

which derives great beauty from the castled hill adorning it on one side, and the bright stream, with the still loftier eminence which skirts it on the other. The streets were perfectly crowded by the students, who, but for their eternal pipes, would be a very fine-looking set of young men. There are some handsome buildings belonging to the University; but I am almost ashamed to confess, that the picturesque fever was so strong upon us at this time, that we made no attempt to see any of the literary and scientific treasures they contain. I think, indeed, that in this town nothing, however pre-eminent in excellence, if it be quite unconnected with the locality, can hope for a due share of notice and admiration. Were I, for instance, a very distinguished personage, and fond of being recognized as such, I would rather seek my honours where I had to contend with all the great ones of the earth, than with the attractions of the crumbling stones, the rugged hills, and shallow stream of Heidelberg.

The next day was devoted to following the Necker, as far as a summer's day and a pair of horses could take us. On quitting the town, by the southern side of the river, we passed under a gateway of some pretension, but no great elegance. The drive, through this narrow valley, to Neckergemund, is as full of beauty as any two or three leagues which any of us remembered. One pretty feature of it is the working of the red-stone quarries, on the opposite side. This continues, at intervals, the whole way; each quarry being divided from its neighbour by jutting crags, too beetling, perhaps, to be worked; but diversified by a beautiful sprinkling of dwarf oak and beech, that contrive to push forth almost horizontally from their fissures. Nothing can be more picturesque than the numerous groups of labourers, employed in blasting, raising, and launching the stones down to the river's edge. This last operation adds no trifling charm to the scene. The continual masses sent from a great height, rolling, bounding, springing, and rattling as they descend, till they finally dash into the water, create a sort of fearful interest by no means unpleasing, when watched from the opposite side of the Necker; but, woe to the unwary wanderer who may chance to take a fancy for rambling on the northern bank! The encountering a train, on the Manchester rail-road, would hardly produce more certain destruction, than would a contact with one of these falling rocks.

The pretty village of Neckergemund hangs, most trinket-like, upon the chain of hills we had followed from Heidelberg. A bright little mountain brook comes dancing down, among its cottages, to join the Necker; and it seems probable, that this brook is sometimes sufficiently copious to occasion a very inconvenient augmentation of the latter stream; for we read, on several houses, inscriptions, recording the height of the water at different periods, in some of which all the lower part of the village must have been submerged.

We here crossed the river,—carriage, horses, and all,—in a flat-bottomed boat, just large enough, and not an inch to spare. The Necker makes a turn at this place, almost at right angles; and, when we were in the middle of the stream, and could command both reaches at once, the view almost suggested the idea of fairy land; so much did the bold, unexpected objects, which became visible, exceed all we had seen, or hoped to see. In looking towards the country we had passed, we observed that the river assumed the appearance of a lovely lake, surrounded on all sides by towering cliffs; and, on turning the eye forward, a lofty, conical, forest-covered hill presented itself, crowned by a circular town, which covers its summit completely. A ruinous, embattled wall surrounds the whole; and a mighty tower, of size most disproportioned to the town it guards, rises magnificently against the sky.

On reaching the left-hand shore, the road continues close to the water's edge; till, at the distance of two miles, the ancient town of Neckersteinach, unquestionably one of the loveliest spots in this most lovely land, appears in sight.

From this point, to the little hotel, to which we had been directed, a distance of about half a mile, we drove through some scenery which really looks as if the objects had been brought together purposely to enchant the eye. The marvellous Tilsberg, with the circular town and lofty tower on its brow, rises steep and abrupt, on the opposite side of the river, from the midst of a little, bright, green, level meadow on its bank. Before us was the rambling town of Neckersteinach, scattered up and down the little hill on which it stands, with about a score of light craft moored before it; and, above our heads, towering rocks and dark forests rose steep and high, with the ruins of two stately castles looking down upon us from among them. On another rising knoll, quite distinct from all the hills around it, stood the dismantled, but less ruinous, remains of two other *bergs;* which seemed to have their strength linked together by walled terraces erected between them. The Necker makes a sudden, but beautiful, sweep round the little meadow at the foot of the Tilsberg; and the curving shore opposite, the boats, the houses, and their hanging gardens, the ruined castles, and the forest-covered height on which they stand, altogether form a picture very seldom equalled. It was just such scenery as one longed to revel in, without the incumbrance of carriage and horses, or anything else to prevent one's turning first this way, and then the other, without any restraint whatever.

We wasted but little time in bespeaking dinner,

giving orders to the driver about our return, and such other ordinary matters, ere we found ourselves climbing the isolated knoll, towards the most curious, though the least ruined, castle of the four. But, before we reached it, another pleasure awaited us; for, on attaining the summit of the little ridge, and looking down upon the side of it, farthest from the Necker, instead of seeing the undulating ground, which generally connects such an elevation with the loftier heights in its vicinity, we beheld a little valley deep sunk below us; so bright in verdure, and so tempting from its cool and quiet shade, that nothing prevented my immediately descending into it but a timely recollection of the labour of returning. Through this emerald valley flowed a stream, rapid, deep, and clear, called the Steinach; which a guide-book describes as "le ruisseau le plus anciennement cité loin à la ronde." If it were *cité* for its exceeding beauty, I can well understand this; for it is just such a stream as an errant knight might wish to reach, when longing to slake his thirst, after a fierce and fiery combat, or to repose his limbs on a velvet turf, under the eternal shade of lofty hills and umbrageous oaks.

After gazing at this miniature valley, till we had sufficiently refreshed ourselves by the sight of its coolness, we proceeded to the castle; which, old records say, was the residence of a powerful baron:—lord, not only of the valley and the stream, but also of the knights, who inhabited the three other strongholds in its neighbourhood, and who held them as his vassals, and for his security. One of these subject knights acquired the name of Landschaden, signifying "curse of the country," or something very like it; which amiable appellation remained with his race, till a few years ago, when the last male died childless. The castle of his chief, though the oldest of the four, and known to have existed in the year 1140, is still in part habitable. The Rittersaal has, probably, been little changed; being still a large handsome room, commanding most lovely views by two large windows, one looking across the Necker towards the Tilsberg, the other to the little valley of the Steinach. In this hall of the knights was seated a person, whom we imagined to be some public functionary, as he had various papers, and implements for writing, before him. He was very civil; and, had he been not quite so old, or not quite so young, I doubt not that the romance, which, from the moment I came in sight of the place, had been gathering before me, like the *mirage* of the desert, would have enabled me to imagine him some very distinguished personage; taking refuge from the malice of fortune, in a spot where nature alone seemed capable of atoning for all the sorrows that the world could bring. But, alas! a middle-aged personage at once puts to sleep, extinguishes, and annihilates all sublime inquiries; so, after obtaining what local information he could give us, we left the Rittersaal, and climbed and dived into every part of the half-ruinous edifice—save one. That defied us; and the girl, who padded about after us with bare feet and staring eyes, assured my son, who was the best German of the party, that no one, in the memory of man, had ever found the way to enter *that tower*.

This was by no means the only instance we met with, in our pertinacious examinations of towers, placed in the midst of mysterious old bergs, where the entrance must have been either by excavated passages from below, or by communications from above; but now so completely removed, as to leave no trace whatever as to where or how they could have been used. I decidedly lean to the subterranean hypothesis; as being not only the most mysterious, but the most reasonable; for I cannot believe that any Landschaden of them all would have contrived his castle in such a sort, as to have rendered scaling-ladders necessary, for his own entrances and exits to and from his tower of strength.

There were several other particulars, in this wild old fortalice, that strangely awakened our curiosity; and more still in its situation, that excited our admiration. Had I time and money, *ad libitum*, I should like to enter into a negociation with the present lord of the land, for the purchase of this site, and the old stones which stand upon it; for I could make, I think, so rarely sweet a dwelling of it, that no English friend, wandering between Heidelberg and Stuttgard, but would like to pay me a visit there.

Wishing to pursue our way to the woods, we contented ourselves with a distant glance of the smaller castle, which stands nearer the town, and immediately followed the upward path leading into the forest, which overhangs the road to Neckersteinach. When seen from below, this forest appears too thick to enter; and the ruins, which look out from amidst it, seem to be perched upon unapproachable cliffs; but the beautiful zigzag track we now took led us gradually higher and higher; till, at length, we found ourselves, not only on a level with, but above, the first ruin. It was, however, only from thence we could approach it; and, even so, the way, if not dangerous, was difficult. Thorns and brambles were to be braved; and the last descent upon it could only be performed by scrambling down three or four feet. This done, we came upon a bit of close-shorn turf;—kept thus neatly, either by the scythe, or cropped by the wild animals of the forest. This had been the fortress of the redoubtable Landschaden, and we were therefore determined to enter it; but, from the point we had reached, there were no means of getting into the only chamber that remained entire, except by crawling on all-fours through a breach in the wall. This we performed, with the proper degree of antiquarian enthusiasm, and found ourselves in a very interesting dungeon, from whence there was no exit, save by the self-same hole through which we had entered.

So far, we had gained but little by our noble daring; but, having crawled out again, we found one or two spots among the heaps of fallen stones, which had once formed the bulwark of the knight of Landschaden, so singularly well placed for commanding a look-out up the river, and down the river, and across to the old frowning Tilsberg, that we understood why this one, at least, of the three dependent bergs was necessary for the protection of their chief.

Here, again, we found a tower not to be entered but by scaling or undermining—and a solid tower it is. We were told that the stones, of which it was constructed, were coveted by some person in the neighbourhood for the purposes of building; but it was found that the labour of separating them from each other would be greater than that of hewing materials from one of the neighbouring quarries. From these dark fragments, we scrambled our way up again to the mountain-path, which now led, by nearly a level terrace, to the fourth castle. This, too, is utterly in decay; but the platform before it, looking down a tremendous precipice, is occupied as a garden by a poor man, who has made his dwelling among the ruins.

At this point, we decided that our party should separate for an hour before dinner; that none might interfere with the occupation of the others. Mr. H——, having spied out some spot, which he thought more beautiful still, to sketch from, set off in that direction. My son mounted up, hammer in hand, to the summit of the rocky heights above our head. And I turned back, to scribble in my note-book, at a point where I thought I could rest greatly to my satisfaction; and where my companions promised to join me. I was not, however, quite alone. My little guide sat on a neighbouring stone, with his elbow resting on his knee; looking down upon the river, and its boats, the town, and its castles, with an air of most happy idleness. A little adventure occurred, while securing his services, which made me look on his contented face with peculiar pleasure. On setting off from the inn, this little fellow stepped up, cap in hand, to make an offer of himself, as our guide to the various ruins. I have constantly found that these little local urchins are excellent in that capacity. They know every mysterious hole and cranny; and have a marvellous talent of helping out their words, in answer to our imperfect German inquiries, with most amusing and expressive grimaces;—so we set off without asking for any other. The young rogue testified his satisfaction, by every imaginable demonstration of glee. He smiled, he laughed, he bowed, as he scampered on before us; but, ere we had gone fifty yards, a boy, more than twice his age, presented himself, and, pushing aside the little one, began to chatter forth his own information, with an air of great importance. We wished to get rid of him, but it was impossible, and we proceeded with our double escort. On reaching the top of the ridge, from whence the Steinach becomes visible, the little fellow stepped eagerly forward to point out the beautiful valley, and its bright clear brook. This was more than the senior could bear; and seizing upon his rival, with no gentle gripe, he thrust him rudely back. The gay smiles of the poor boy gave place to a burst of tears; whereupon I instantly found German enough to make my election clearly understood: " Nein geld für sie," was sufficient to make the elder stalk off, and my little man remained master of the field. I never witnessed a prettier ebullition of happiness than this triumph produced. He has bowed his merry head every time I have looked at him; gathered every flower in our path to present to me; and, in short, made me feel exceedingly well pleased with myself, for having protected the weak against the strong.

After enjoying, for about an hour, the beautiful seat I had chosen, our man of science, and our man of art returned, and we all repaired together to the inn. What the little, remote town of Neckersteinach can have to do with a ball-room, I cannot imagine; but our very good dinner was set forth in a *saal*, of excellent dimensions for a waltz of fifty couple, with a fine, glittering, glass chandelier, suspended in the middle of it. It required some resolution to leave this airy room, with its double range of beautiful windows, to plunge again into the sunshine; and still more, to decide upon climbing the almost perpendicular side of the Tilsberg, in order to examine the singular buildings on its top. I mustered courage, however, for the undertaking; and crossed the Necker, to the bright green meadow on its opposite shore. Had I been quite aware how very long this walk up the Tilsberg would have been, I should probably have requested my companions to undertake it without me; yet I gloried in the enterprise, when it was achieved; both from the satisfaction of having performed a difficult task, and for the strange, wild, desolate aspect of the curious place we had reached. The view was most magnificent. We looked down upon the ruined castles, and their little heights, as if they had been toys; and the valley of the Necker spread itself, like a map, for several miles, on both sides. As to the town itself, and the ruins of its immense castle, it would be very difficult to give any idea of either. Their form and position are very singular. The town is so nearly in ruins, and the few hovels, which continue to be inhabited, are so extremely wretched in appearance, that I should think they would, at no very distant period, be as utterly forsaken by the peasants, who still cling to them, as the castle has been by the knight who held it. Yet, few and poor as the inhabitants are, they have still a decent little Catholic church; and their piety shows itself by many tiny offerings to the Virgin, pinned about her shrine. A few inches of narrow ribbon, or a scrap of muslin, or silk, had not been thought too paltry to offer, or too worthless to accept; and, though flowers could not be found round their desolate dwellings, they had plucked green branches from the forest which clothes the isolated hill, and with these the altar was decorated. The only dwelling in the place, which appeared calculated to be a shelter for man, was a small tenement, close to the church: it was in no respect superior to the cottages which poor men inhabit in the world below; but, amidst the ruins of Tilsberg, it had an air of superiority, which led us to imagine, that, if there were a priest in the place, he must dwell there. We judged rightly. On applying at the door, for permission to enter the church, it was the curé himself who answered us; and who had the politeness to unlock the door, and show us the little all it contained. He informed us, however, that this lonely spot was not his dwelling-place; but that he came once or twice a week to perform mass, and to administer to the spiritual wants of the poor people.

On the whole, though I am certainly pleased to have seen this very remarkable village, I do not recommend the expedition to my travelling readers; particularly if they be ladies, for it is a most fatiguing one. Let them contemplate the Tilsberg from the lovely woods of Neckersteinach; and they will see enough of its singular position to gratify their curiosity, without paying the penalty of so much weariness.

When preparing for our return, we got outside the walls, and were obliged to cling round them, almost as cautiously as if walking on the parapet of a house; so completely does the exterior of the town reach the edge of the small table-land on which it is built. In one direction only is there an approach less precipitous, and this is on the side farthest from the Necker.

While recrossing the river on our return, we were much struck by the beautiful appearance of the Steinach brook, where it runs into the Necker. I have seen the clear Ohio join the muddy Mississippi; and, still more to the purpose, I have seen that turbid stream rush among the bright blue waves of the Mexican gulf; and, in both instances, there is a very tardy mixture of their waters;—but the pertinacious purity of the sparkling little Steinach is more remarkable than either. It flows gaily and swiftly through the gentle descent of its own valley; but, just where it joins the Necker, it comes down with a vehemence which carries it pure and pellucid, for a longer distance than I could have believed possible, before it is stained and lost in the stronger and coarser stream.

We greatly enjoyed the cool evening drive back to Heidelberg. It had all that beautiful variety of light and shade which a brilliant sunset gives, in a region of high cliffs and deep valleys.

We passed, on our return, two or three of the

rafts by which the timber of the black forest is conveyed to the Rhine. These were small, and had only two or three men on each of them; but, when they reach the Rhine, so prodigious a number of them are linked together, that they proceed to Rotterdam, rather like mighty floating islands, thickly peopled, than a paltry combination of logs.

The following day, which was to be the last of our stay at Heidelberg, was devoted to a deliberate examination of its ruins, and to the quiet enjoyment of the matchless terraces and gardens around them.

I have already said so much about these ruins, that I almost fear to give any account of this day; but, recollecting how easy a matter it is to turn over a few pages at once, I shall venture to transcribe, verbatim, from my note-book what I wrote at the time; in the hope that it may recal to some, who love every tower and staircase of the old place as well as I do, recollections that may have escaped their memory.

Ruins of Heidelberg, July, 1833.

We are here to pass the whole day. The *valet de place* has brought a basket of provisions from the hotel; and we have found German enough to persuade a young damsel to take charge of it, who resides with her father, the *tonnelier* of the castle, under shelter of one of the various roofs which still remain of this palace of wonders. They have contrived to give an air of comfort to a part of the offices, divided off into three or four snug little rooms. What the exact meaning of the good man's title may be, I do not well understand; for all the *cooperage* of the castle, at this time, consists in preserving the celebrated "*Tun of Heidelberg*" from premature decay. But, whatever be his office, it seems to support him in very comfortable style; and his "neat-handed" daughter is a model of good-humoured notability. With true German kindness, she has received our basket, and furnished us with chairs, to carry with us to any part of the castle in which we may choose to station ourselves.

Henry has just been fortunate enough to meet one of the most distinguished geologists of the day, who has had the kindness to tell him of some object of peculiar interest, at the distance of a mile;

and for this, he and his hammer are about to depart. Mr. H. is already seated, pencil in hand, before the Rittersaal; with the ambitious project of conveying on paper some idea of its elaborate splendour:—and I shall convey my note-book about with me into every quarter of this extraordinary place: —not, certainly, with any expectation of being able to describe what I may see, but for the purpose of making a memorandum from time to time of my enjoyment; in the hope that I may induce others to adopt the same satisfactory mode of proceeding.

* * * * * * *

My first perambulation has brought me to a grove of stately forest trees, growing on the old ramparts of the castle. Through this grove walks are cut, and still kept with the nicest care.

On one side is the castle ditch,—deep, dark, and filled with trees, whose tops are on a level with me. On the other, the wall of the bastion sinks perpendicularly, for a hundred feet; and the bold hill, on which it rests, continues the precipice in a line not much more practicable. At its foot lies the town of Heidelberg, with its busy market; where the crowds, whom I saw buying and selling as I passed through it, now look like so many bustling ants carrying their tiny loads. Luckily for me there is a stout iron rail, fixed in the massy stone-work, or I could not thus stand on its edge to watch them. The Necker stretches far away along the rich valley which conducts it to the Rhine; and the blue line of the Vosges, extending to Mont Tonnerre, finishes the distance.

All this may, I think, be easily imagined; for mountains often have castles on their sides, and rivers and towns at their base. But only those who have been here—here, on the very spot where I now stand—can form a just idea of the actual scene. Close beside me rise the walls of an immense tower, whose span is so ample, that its four windows, overlooking this terrace, seem but slightly bowed. Below these windows, and standing forth from the ivy which has crept round their projecting niches, are the highly-finished, full-length statues of the two founders of the tower:—the Elector Lewis V., and his brother Frederick V. Their embroidered cloaks, their stiff ruffs, and all the minutiæ of their stately toilet, are so accurately given, and so well preserved, that a very little fancy might enable one to believe in their having been petrified, lace and all, as they were stepping down from the balcony above. The ivy around these figures has been very skilfully cut; and they appear to be pushing it aside to enable them to look down upon the terrace.

This part of the structure is called *par excellence* " the Great Tower;" and in it was the famous banqueting hall of Frederick V. On a tablet of stone placed between the two Electors is an inscription, of which the following is a translation :—

" Lewis, Count Palatine of the Rhine, Elector and Duke of Bavaria, erected this tower, and finished it in 1583.

" Frederick V., Count Palatine of the Rhine, Elector, Vicar of the Holy Roman Empire, and Duke of Bavaria, pulled down the upper part of this tower, rebuilt, and vaulted it; and added thirty-three feet to the height of the banqueting hall, after having removed the column which supported the roof, without any damage or derangement whatever. Finished in the year 1619." This magnificent tower is connected with the building which contains the chapel by a simple, but very noble range of apartments, called " the English Buildings." These were erected in 1612, by Frederick V., for the especial use of his wife, the Princess Elizabeth of England, daughter of James I. The windows of two lofty stories are still remaining; and this enormous wall, seen together with the mighty tower, which flanks it, against the clear, blue sky of Germany, conveys an idea of immensity and grandeur which cannot be described. Nature and art both appear gigantic here; for, turning to the right, a hill of such sudden steepness rises to the clouds, while the trees which cover it are so noble, and the masses of rock starting forth from among them so enormous, that the style of the building seems chosen on purpose to be in keeping with the stupendous features of the landscape.

Many parts of the castle have reference, by their history, or by inscriptions, to the Princess Elizabeth of England. Over the arch of what must have been a very noble gateway, leading to this terrace, is the following inscription:—

"Frederick the Fifth to his dear wife Elizabeth, in the year 1615."

*　　*　　*　　*　　*　　*

I have now got into the very deepest recesses of the ruin. I have climbed up one very long spiral staircase, and sounded my way down another. After this, I had the good fortune to find a third, darker and narrower than either; and, having mastered it, I found myself amidst a labyrinth of paths, running along the tops of the walls of Otho Henry's palace. Fortunately they are, one and all, broad enough to make a very respectable promenade. Moreover, many of them are guarded by bushes springing from the mortar; and along others a slight *garde-fou* has been placed, that curiosity might not lead to danger, nor fear to disappointment. After threading these paths till, spite of the rails and the bushes, I found myself sufficiently giddy, and perfectly bewildered, I at length made my way to what my map tells me is the "Tour de la Bibliothèque:"—and here I write, seated on what seems the hearthstone of Frederick the Second, who is said to have built this splendid chamber to contain the famous library of the Palatinate;—one of the most valuable collections then existing. The room must, I think, have been a half circle. It has eight large windows, among which it is difficult to select that which commands the most enchanting view. Some look down the side of the hill, over terraces and covered ways, orchards, and forest trees, to the river, the town, and its pigmy population. Others open upon the towering Geisberg:— and it is not without an effort that you can get sight of the blue sky above it. From one of them are seen the noble range of windows at the back of Otho Henry's palace, behind the famous Ritter-saal; and beyond these again, is the octagon tower, which is the highest fragment left; and which is visible at many points where no other part of the ruins can be seen. The floor of this room is now, perhaps, more softly carpeted than in the days of its greatness; for a well-kept, green-grass turf covers it. A stunted, leafless shrub stands in the centre;

just on the spot where, formerly, some massy oaken table probably supported the precious manuscripts and illuminated missals, when they were brought forth to regale the eyes of the learned visitants to this princely library. The noble Elector himself must have intended to use this room as a favourite apartment; for the building is so arranged as to communicate, by a small vaulted closet, with the chamber of Otho's palace, called " the Elector's Bed-room;" and from this closet a little spiral staircase leads to the ground floor. A subterranean passage communicates, from a point near this tower, with an entrance at a very considerable distance in the side of the Jettenbuhl.

* * * * * *

Henry has found out my retreat; he assures me that the hour of dinner is fully come, and that we must find some spot of transcendent beauty, whereat to assemble for the purpose of making our repast. The only difficulty will be in choosing among such vast variety. I think, at least, an hundred different parties might find spots of first-rate attraction, where they might place themselves, without interfering with each other.

* * * * * *

After due consideration, we have decided upon the matchless northern terrace, outside the chapel, for our dinner station. It overhangs the town and river, and looks over them to the Heiligenberg; as one good neighbour does to another, across a narrow street. Here, in the deep shade of Frederick the Fourth's lofty palace,—with one stone bench for our table, and another for our seat,—we have spread our repast. It is a banqueting-hall which might content the most fastidious prince on earth.

* * * * * *

Having eaten, and looked about us for at least one long, but not unsatisfactory hour, we went in search of the person who keeps the keys of the chapel, the picture gallery, the chamber of the *Great Tun,* and various other curiosities, by the exhibition of which she contrives to get a living. The chapel of St. Udalrich is the part of the castle which has undergone the latest reparation; and it was used as late as the year 1803. It makes part of

Frederick the Fourth's palace, and is large enough to have assorted well with the dignity of the entire building; but now it has only its bare walls and naked altar to show, and possesses little other interest than what is derived from its being part of the ruins of Heidelberg.

There is, however, one strange object there,—wherefore, or by whom placed, I know not,—but it deserves mention, were it only for the startling effect it produced on us all. On entering the chapel we passed by the side of an old confessional, placed near the door;—it had neither dignity nor beauty of any kind to attract the eye, and it was quite unheeded. On reaching the altar, we turned to examine the extent of the building; and, at the same moment, the eyes of each of us were drawn to the figure of a pale old man, who, dressed in the habit of a monk, sat in the confessional we had passed. There was something so desolate in the look of the place, and so unearthly in the livid hue of his complexion, that I almost shuddered as I looked at him. He seemed to bend his head meekly towards us, as in salutation; and a strong feeling of interest and compassion was excited in us all; for it appeared as if he alone had survived the universal wreck in which all around him had perished, and that, faithful to his duty even to the last—for his hollow eye and sunken cheek showed that life was fast ebbing—he still held his post, to minister comfort to the repentant spirits who might yet hover near to confess their sins. The woman, who had led us into the chapel, watched us earnestly as we continued to gaze upon him; and, after the silence of a moment, said, "Go up to him."

We all obeyed her; and it was not till we found ourselves close to the confessional that we discovered this excellent mockery to be of wax.

From the chapel, we passed on to a building which has the honour of containing the Great Tun of Heidelberg. This celebrated cask is certainly very large; and the idea, that it was wont in days of yore to be filled with Rhine wine, approaches to the sublime;—but before I could fully appreciate its dignity, Henry quite destroyed the effect of all its greatness, by exclaiming,—"A dozen of them might dance in Meux's great vat!"

We next visited a queer collection of pictures, kept in a room over the great gateway. It consists, almost entirely, of portraits of the princes and princesses of the Palatinate, to whom the castle has at different periods belonged. After we had sufficiently examined these, Mr. H—— returned to his drawing, and Henry and I set off in search of vaulted dungeons, and subterranean passages. Of these we found many more than we could follow, or even enter. The particular spot which, more than any other, possesses this kind of interest, is, perhaps, that beneath the stupendous ruin of the circular tower which fronts the Geeisberg. The manner in which the upper half of this tower now lies extended on the ground,—the solid mass of its enormous walls still preserving their circular form, while the lower half yawns beside it,—presents one of the greatest charms of the whole ruin ; and the vaults beneath are in the very highest style of dark and dreary mystery. It was quite impossible, however, even for Henry, to penetrate quite as far as might have been wished for the gratification of that curiosity, which, on such occasions, grows by what it feeds on ; but, on the whole, we were well satisfied with the result of the accuracy of our researches, so far as they had proceeded; and, when the failing light admonished us to desist, we congratulated each other upon having dived farther into the hidden recesses of Heidelberg than it was likely any other travellers had done before us.

When we returned to the front of the Rittersaal, where we had left Mr. H——, we found him in conversation with a French artist, who has devoted the last twenty-three years of his life to making drawings, and superintending engravings, of all the most interesting parts of the ruin. Some of these, especially such as give the detail of Otho Henry's superb façade, are admirable.

This gentleman, by name M. Charles de Graimberg, gave us many amusing anecdotes of occurrences which had passed under his notice, during his long residence among these noble relics. He has had the opportunity of witnessing the impressions produced by them on a great variety of travellers of all nations; and this, I think, must have left on his memory a sort of patchwork recollection of high and low feeling—of extravagant enthusiasm and cold indifference—which may enable him to judge of the average taste of mankind better than most people.

I believe it was this gentleman who told me that a set of learned and most energetic English antiquaries, having worshipped these remains of German magnificence during the day, returned to them, in the darkness of night, armed with sledge hammers, and testified their love of art by severing sundry fragments of stone from the beautiful ornaments of the Rittersaal.

Notwithstanding the pleasure they had given us, our affection for the caryatides, the corbels, and the cornices did not lead us to go this length; and we left the ruin of Heidelberg, carrying away with us nothing, save the remembrance of its surpassing beauty.

When we returned to our inn we were too tired to do anything but sit still and drink coffee; but the evening was beautiful, and, till a late hour, the streets were thronged with students, who gave us in passing many delightful specimens of their skill in singing. One large party, who perhaps had been quaffing some few flasks of Rhenish, in honour of the belles of Heidelberg, came carolling down the street, with such a preponderating force of lungs, that all weaker strains gave way before them; and then we had a very beautiful example of one of the most characteristic features of Germany. All those, who met this long array of wassailers stretching across the street and suffering nobody to be heard but themselves, instead of breaking their harmony, as they broke their line in passing through it, joined the joyous chorus; with tune, time, and taste so admirable as to produce an effect inconceivably delightful. This did not happen once only, or twice or thrice; but, as they pursued their walk through the street, every party they met joined voices, in most sweet and skilful accord, to the strain they were singing.

END OF VOL. I.

www.ingramcontent.com/pod-product-compliance
Lightning Source LLC
Chambersburg PA
CBHW080432110426
42743CB00016B/3147